Second Edition

Gender Diversity

Second Edition

Gender Diversity

Crosscultural Variations

Serena Nanda

John Jay College of Criminal Justice

WAVELAND
PRESS, INC.

Long Grove, Illinois

For information about this book, contact:
Waveland Press, Inc.
4180 IL Route 83, Suite 101
Long Grove, IL 60047-9580
(847) 634-0081
info@waveland.com
www.waveland.com

Cover Photograph: Kathoey, or transgendered males, are featured perform-ers in transvestite revues in Thailand. (Photograph by Ravinder Nanda.)

10-digit ISBN 1-4786-1126-X
13-digit ISBN 978-1-4786-1126-4

Printed in the United States of America

7   6   5   4   3   2

If we are to achieve a richer culture, rich in contrasting values, we must recognize the whole gamut of human potentialities . . . one in which each diverse human gift will find a fitting place.

— Margaret Mead

Contents

Contents

Preface

This book, based on ethnographic data from many different cultures, is an introduction to the subject of sex/gender diversity. It is aimed at students in gender studies, human sexuality, cultural anthropology, and gay, lesbian, and transgender studies. The ethnographic material is set in the context of the main theoretical issues that inform the contemporary study of sex/gender diversity, which are outlined in the Introduction and summarized in the final chapter. Since the time the first edition was published, there has been an explosion of both theory and ethnographic data on sex and gender diversity, accounting for the decision to publish a second edition. In addition to updating the glossary (boldfaced-italicized terms in the text are listed in the glossary), the references, and the annotated filmography, I have updated most of the chapters, included new data on hijras in Bangladesh, added a new chapter on Indonesia, and introduced a brief section on globalization in the final chapter, "Variations on a Theme." Also new to this edition is a "Review and Reflection" section at the end of chapters 1–8. Each section is designed to reinforce an understanding of concepts specific to that chapter and also to motivate readers to compare and contrast them with those discussed in other chapters, allowing for broader, crosscultural reflection.

This book is made possible because of the outstanding ethnographies and histories that have been published on gender diversity in the last 30 years. These authors are identified in the text and have my unstinting admiration. I am also profoundly grateful to my family, friends, and colleagues who have encouraged my own work in gender diversity and have been so generous in sharing their ideas and photographs with me: Jasper Burns, Sharyn (Graham) Davies, Joan Gregg, Kelley Hayes, Gilbert Herdt, Adnan Hossain, Gabriela Magerl, Martin

Manalansan IV, Ravinder Nanda, Jill Norgren, Russell Oberlin, Michael Peletz, Jill Peters, Gayatri Reddy, John Reid, Will Roscoe, Tanti Noor Said, Michael Sweet, Randolph Trumbach, Unni Wikan, Walter Williams, and Sam Winter. I am particularly grateful to my dear friend and colleague, Niko Besnier, who not only has made an outstanding contribution to the fields of gender studies and gender diversity but also gave so generously of his time and energy to respond to all my many queries in the course of writing this revision. I also wish to thank Caroline Brettell, Richley Crapo, and Alice Kehoe for their thoughtful and helpful reviews of the original manuscript.

I am grateful to the PSC-CUNY Research Foundation for the partial funding of my fieldwork on the hijras; the Park Ridge Center for the Study of Health, Faith, and Ethics in Chicago for funding my participation in their symposium on Religion and Sexuality; and to the library staff and the Anthropology Department at John Jay College of Criminal Justice, particularly Joanie Ward and Luis Talledo, for their essential support services. Jeni Ogilvie, my editor at Waveland, was immeasurably helpful, and I am very appreciative of her contribution. She is a pleasure to work with. Finally, I want to thank Tom Curtin of Waveland Press, a longtime friend and colleague. Through his commitment to presenting anthropological research to undergraduate students in an interesting and accessible format, Tom and Waveland Press make an invaluable contribution to the discipline of cultural anthropology.

Introduction

In contemporary Euro-American cultures binary opposites—male and female, man and woman, homosexual and heterosexual, indeed the binary opposition of sex and gender itself—are central to the dominant gender ideology. The male/female binary appears as a basic, perhaps even universal, pattern in human society (see Quinn and Luttrell 2004). At the same time many societies contain sex/gender roles that transcend this binary opposition, making it clear that both sex and gender are culturally constructed. Since the first edition of this book was published, there has been a proliferation of terms to describe **sex/gender diversity**—sex/gender roles that transcend the binary opposition of male and female; man and woman. (For "sex/gender diversity," I also interchangeably use "sex/gender variation," "alternative sex/genders," "nonnormative sex/gender roles," "liminal sex/gender roles," and "transgenderism," as these are used in the most recent ethnographies.)

Ethnographic research on sex/gender diversity is significant in its own right and important in gender studies more generally. Anthropology's crosscultural approach enables us to think about behavior, attitudes, and perceptions and identities relating to sex, gender, and sexuality that are not part of our own experience. The anthropological perspective also cautions us against making any easy generalizations about "human nature." Because sex, gender, and sexuality are at the very core of individual identity in modern Western culture, it is difficult to dislodge our ideas, and more so, our feelings, about them. The examples of sex/gender diversity in this book challenge intellectual understandings about what is natural, normal, and morally right and also challenge us at deeper emotional and personal levels.

A crosscultural perspective makes it clear that there are many different ways that societies organize their thinking about sex, gender,

1

and sexuality. All the cultures described here provide spaces for sex and gender roles beyond the binary opposites of male and female, man and woman; perhaps sex/gender diversity, like the sex/gender binary, is also universal. There are both similarities and differences among these roles, all of which are influenced by specific histories, cultural patterns, and social and political contexts. This is illustrated by the substantial changes in these roles and societal response, in the modern era, through culture contact, colonialism, and contemporary globalization.

The cultures represented here do not encompass the total range of sex/gender diversity. Some important examples, such as the male transgendered *xanith* of Oman (Wikan 1977), woman–woman marriage and female husbands in Africa (Amadiume 1987; Oboler 1980; Roscoe and Murray 1998), nonnormative sex/gender roles in West Africa (Gaudio 2009), historically important sex/gender diversity in Southeast Asia (Peletz 2009), and transgender roles in Mesoamerica (Marcos 2002) and Asia (Winter 2013) are regretfully omitted due to space limitations. I chose my examples because they are ethnographically well documented and because they represent diverse geographical areas and diverse cultural patterns of sex and gender.

SOME BASIC DEFINITIONS

In order to understand sex/gender diversity, a grasp of some basic issues and definitions is necessary. **Sex** refers to the biologically differentiated status of male or female. It includes anatomic sex, particularly the genitals, and also secondary and invisible characteristics such as genes and hormones. **Gender** refers to the social, cultural, and psychological constructions that are imposed on the biological differences of sex.

The distinction between sex and gender as developed by social scientists has been useful in challenging the view that biological sex determines the roles and attributes of men and women in society. Social scientists viewed biological sex (the opposition of male and female) as "natural" and universal, and gender (the opposition of man and woman) as culturally constructed and variable. Thus, this differentiation between sex and gender made an important contribution in undermining biological determinism, especially in the study of women's roles. Nevertheless, the dichotomy is now being challenged on the basis that biological sex is also an idea constructed only through culture (see especially Butler 1990:6; Karkazis 2008).

The ethnographic record makes clear that there is no simple, universal, inevitable, or "correct" correspondence between sex and gender and that the Euro-American privileging of biological sex (anatomy) is not universal; many cultures do not even make the distinction between the natural and the cultural or between sex and gender. In many societies anatomical sex is not the dominant factor in constructing gender roles and gender identity. In addition, opposing the terms "sex" and "gender" overlooks the integration of biology and culture in human life, experience, and behavior. Thus, I generally use the term "sex/gender," unless the opposition of sex and gender is an explicit and significant element in the cultural pattern under discussion.

   Sexuality, another critical concept in the study of *gender diversity* (*gender variation*), refers to erotic desires, sexual practices, or sexual orientation. Western understandings of sexuality have been inappropriately imposed on other cultures. This is particularly true regarding *homosexuality* (desire for the same). In contemporary Euro-American culture individuals are socially identified as homosexuals or *heterosexuals* (desire for the other) as if one's *sexual orientation* encapsulated one's total personality and identity. In contrast to this cultural pattern, "the homosexual" and "the heterosexual" as social identities do not exist in many societies, where "same" sexual desire and relations go largely unacknowledged. In addition, many cultures do not identify both partners in same-sex sexual relations as homosexual but only the partner whose sexual role is opposite to his or her anatomy. Thus, in male same-sex sexual relationships only the partner who takes the receptor role in anal or oral sex is culturally marked, and the "male" or active partner is not considered different from other men. In some cultures, in a pattern called *gendered homosexuality*, each of the partners in a same-sex relationship enacts the role of either a man or a woman, patterned on conventional gender roles in that culture, and may be reclassified as to their sex/gender status (Murray 1995:11).

   This text is *not* about homosexuality in its contemporary Euro-American sense as an identity shared by all persons whose preference is for sexual partners of the same sex. Rather, this text is about sex/gender diversity, whose relation to sexuality varies across cultures. The frequent Euro-American misidentification of gender diversity with homosexuality has led to misunderstandings of alternative sex/gender roles in other cultures. At the same time, contemporary globalization has led to a diffusion of some Western sex/gender concepts, like gay and lesbian, though these have different meanings in different cultures.

   Sex/gender diversity varies both among and within cultures. While all of the variant sex/gender roles described in this text are linguistically differentiated from the normative gender roles of man and woman, some of these variant roles are relatively more coherent and well defined—that is, more *institutionalized*—than others. Cultures also vary in the extent to which gender diversity has sacred or spiritual associations: In India, gender transformations are considered inherently powerful or auspicious, while in Polynesia and the United States, alternative sex/gender roles are basically secular.

Sex/gender roles and identities must always be analyzed in connection with other cultural patterns: most important, the dominant sex/gender ideology, but also other factors such as class, race, and age. Even in multigendered cultures, gender diversity always exists against a background of what it means to be male or female, man or woman in a particular society. In addition, while broader cultural patterns illuminate the meanings of sex/gender diversity, understandings of sex/gender diversity also illuminate other aspects of culture. We see this in Bangladesh and Brazil, for example, where nonnormative male roles illuminate norms of masculinity, but normative masculine gender roles also illuminate male transgender roles.

SOCIAL ATTITUDES TOWARD SEX/GENDER DIVERSITY

Relatively speaking, sex/gender variance has not been as severely sanctioned in non-Western cultures as it has been in the West. While some Western writing perhaps overidealizes and romanticizes the acceptance of sex/gender diversity in other cultures, such societies do seem to provide a space for sex/gender variant roles, allow wide latitude for the expression of sex/gender variation, and more easily integrate sex/gendered variant individuals into the social structure. Nonetheless, certainly in most contemporary societies, such individuals are often ambivalently regarded and may be marginalized, stigmatized, discriminated against, criminalized, and even subjected to violence. Attitudes toward sex/gender diversity may include awe, fear, respect, ridicule, disgust, dismay, pity, or bemusement, and tolerance is not the same as approval or legitimacy. Even in societies like India and Brazil, or in Southeast Asia, where gender diversity has traditionally been associated with ritual powers, attitudes toward gender variants in ordinary social interaction are frequently ambivalent and sometimes even hostile. Furthermore, a tolerant or positive attitude toward gender diversity in the past does not necessarily translate into acceptance of gender diversity in the present. Historically, for example, Native American societies often valued gender diversity, but contemporary gay and lesbian individuals may face stigma and discrimination on Native American reservations.

Hostile social attitudes toward gender diversity, specialized occupations associated with gender variants, and other factors, such as social class, may lead to the spatial segregation of gender variants and/or the development of subcultures and social communities, as in Indian, Brazilian, Filipino, and some European cities. The degree to which gender diversity is associated with spatially bounded social groups or specialized subcultures may be a function of a society's population size, religion, political structure, or discrimination based on occupation, particularly prostitution.

Attitudes toward sex/gender diversity vary within cultures as well as between them. Age, region, social class, educational level, ethnicity, religion, urban or rural residence, exposure to Western cultures, and gender itself are all factors influencing attitudes toward gender diversity. In addition, social attitudes toward sex/gender diversity are often built on stereotypes and are somewhat different than attitudes sex/gender variant individuals have about themselves, especially when social attitudes are negative. While cultural images of sex/gender diversity do influence how individuals see themselves, there are also important individual differences in *sex/gender identity*—how one experiences oneself as a sexed and gendered person. This individual variation is based on differences in personality, life circumstances, social class, and other factors and helps explain variation in recruitment to gender variant roles and in public presentation. Individuals vary in how they play alternatively gendered roles and how they challenge or manipulate cultural norms as they try to adapt to their societies.

While sex/gender diversity describes cultural categories, it is also a matter of personal identity. Ethnographic research resoundingly demonstrates that even individuals included in the same alternative sex/gender categories often experience themselves differently. And although the term "identity" implies a certain consistency or continuity in subjective experience, identities are dynamic; they change with the situation or over time, affected by both social and individual factors. Even the most institutionalized sex/gender identities are always more varied than a focus on cultural norms alone would imply. Individual identities encapsulated in personal narratives (which may also include those of anthropologists) that are particularly helpful for further research are featured in the selected films list and are indicated by the asterisk (*) placed after the ethnographies listed in the reference section.

SEXUALITY AND GENDER DIVERSITY

Significant cultural variation occurs in what is considered appropriate sexuality—desire, orientation, practices—for different genders and in the presumed relationship between sex/gender diversity, sexuality, and gender identity. Sexual orientation, for example, is an important part of personal and social identity in contemporary Euro-American cultures but is no longer as closely associated with diverse gender roles as it was in the eighteenth, nineteenth, and early-twentieth centuries. In Brazil sexuality is central to gender variance, but it is sexual practice—position in sexual intercourse—more than sexual orientation that determines one's place in the sex/gender system. This is also true to some extent in Thailand and the Philippines. In contrast, in Polynesia and among Native Americans, sexuality is less important than occupation in defining sex/gender diversity, while in India, in medieval Europe, and the Balkans, the renunciation of sexuality is, ideally, culturally central in defining both male and female gender variant roles. In Indonesia sex/gender diversity includes several alternative sex/gender roles, each of which occupies a different social status.

The frequent association of male gender diversity with prostitution and sexual "deviance," especially as part of an international sex work industry, complicates the picture of crosscultural male gender variant sexuality. Western researchers have generally underestimated and underreported the role of sexual desire in commercial sex, viewing prostitution as if it were a simple "selling of the body." Although we can never overlook the association of prostitution with poverty, the exchange of sex for money is culturally variable and needs also to be viewed as part of a complex system of culturally motivated transactions in which symbolic and emotional exchanges are relevant.

Nevertheless, the association between prostitution and gender variant males compounds social hostility toward these individuals, as does the presumed association between sex/gender diversity and AIDS. At the same time, the association with Westerners that sex work often entails may bring some prestige in non-Western nations. The income from prostitution is also sometimes translated into symbols of high social status or used to gain social acceptance within the families of gender variants, who may lean on them for economic support.

GLOBALIZATION AND GENDER DIVERSITY

Culture contact is an important source of change in sex/gender ideologies and identities. The first European encounters with non-European cultures all affected indigenous sex/gender ideologies and roles; in some places, as in parts of Southeast Asia, Native American societies, and Hawai'i, gender diversity was practically destroyed, though most recently it is being revived. The diffusion of Euro-American culture continues today through tourism (including international sex tourism), the global media, the Internet, the spread of academic and scientific discourses, and an activist international human rights agenda.

In all the cultures described in this book, Euro-American sex/gender identities, such as "gay" and "lesbian," have become incorporated into traditional sex/gender ideologies, though often in ways that change their original meanings. This incorporation of Western ideas means that in most societies today several sex/gender systems—indigenous and foreign, traditional and modern—operate simultaneously, with gender variant individuals moving between and among them as they try to construct their lives in meaningful and positive ways.

Cultural influences spread in many directions, however. The sex/gender ideologies of other cultures also influence those of the West, significantly through the medium of anthropological representation. The ethnographic evidence that sex/gender identities and roles are understood differently in different cultures has found its way back into Euro-American societies and is an important source of contemporary transgender and gay rights movements. Crosscultural knowledge has also led to the increasing willingness of the larger society to understand, and perhaps even appreciate, sex/gender diversity.

FEMALE GENDER DIVERSITY

Reflecting the more extensive ethnographic and historical record, this text mainly describes patterns of male sex/gender diversity. For reasons that are not completely clear but involve (among others) child-rearing patterns, patriarchy, and biology, male gender variance is more frequently culturally emphasized than female gender variance (but see Blackwood and Wieringa 1999). The anthropological literature, for example, suggests that "achieving manhood" is more difficult than "achieving womanhood" (see Chodorow 1974; Gilmore 1990; Herdt 1981). In patriarchal societies, the social status gained by alternatively gendered women appears less threatening to society than the social status lost by alternatively gendered men; this may partly account for the cultural focus on male gender nonconformity (Bullough and Bullough 1993:46). In addition, constructing contemporary "masculinist" national ideologies may result in more notice, surveillance, and restriction on public presentations of nonnormative male sexuality or gender roles (Boellstorff 2004b).

Furthermore, some of the ethnographic and historical emphasis on male gender variance results from gender bias, as male researchers (or observers) may be denied access to females and/or have less interest in recording their behavior. In early modern Europe, for example, male sodomy was a crime that left a rich archive of court records; this is not available for women, whose same-sex sexual relations were not as severely legally sanctioned. In addition, in many cultures "manly" behavior by females can be incorporated within the culturally defined roles of women in a way that is not true for men; in some cultures, for example Polynesia, elderly women are treated like men.

For the cultures described here, female gender variant roles were found most frequently in Native American societies, though not as frequently as for males; in India, a female gender variant role is described, though such roles are much less visible and less widespread than male roles. In Polynesia, women can be included in the gender variant category, although this is almost completely unrecorded in the historical and anthropological literature (Besnier 1996). In Thailand gender diversity was historically associated with females as well as males but is now associated mainly with males.

In Euro-American cultures, transsexualism, once a category reserved for males, now includes an increasing number of females, as does the latest form of gender diversity, transgenderism. In the Euro-American chapter, I describe two female gender variant roles, both of which center on virginity, one from the European Middle Ages and the other from nineteenth- and early-twentieth-century Balkan culture. Female same-sex sexual desire and practices are normally less visible than those of men but are now getting greater attention, as described in the section on lesbi relations in Indonesia. Despite descriptive gaps, the ethnographic data make clear that female sex/gender diversity has its own cultural dynamic and is not simply a derivative, a parallel, or the reverse of male gender diversity.

BOOK OUTLINE

Chapter 1, "Multiple Genders among Native Americans" surveys gender variance in Native North America as it was documented in 1860–1930. Gender variant roles, related both to religion and occupation, existed throughout the Americas, though most classic anthropological analysis applies to North America. Native North American societies appear to have supported the widest range of genuine multigender systems, though the extent and explanation of such sex/gender diversity is a source of debate.

Chapter 2 describes the male gender variant role of the hijras in India and Bangladesh, and the sādhin, a female gender variant role in India. Hijra and sādhin are both ideologically grounded in the Hindu religious tradition of asceticism, which includes the rule of sexual renunciation, though few hijras actually follow this rule. The new material on hijras in Bangladesh provides a different perspective on hijras' sexuality as well as examines this role in the context of a Muslim majority nation, as compared to Hindu dominated India.

Brazil, described in chapter 3, is an extension of the "Mediterranean" pattern of gendered homosexuality, in which gender is experienced in the sexual distinction between those who penetrate and those who are penetrated. Sex/gender diversity primarily operates in secular contexts in Brazil but also has ritual associations within Afro-Brazilian religions.

Chapter 4 describes male transgender roles in Polynesia. In contrast to the religious and institutionalized nature of sex/gender diversity in Native North America, India, Bangladesh, Brazil, and Indonesia, in Polynesia sex/gender diversity is less institutionalized and largely defined by secular public performances.

Secular performance is also central to sex/gender diversity in contemporary Thailand and the Philippines, described in chapter 5. Additionally, in both societies, sex/gender diversity is mainly constructed as male transgendered homosexuality. Both nations have been significantly influenced by Western culture and are today characterized by multiple sex/gender ideologies, including a concept of "gay," that sometimes overlap or contradict each other.

Chapter 6 is a new chapter on sex/gender diversity in Indonesia, whose traditional acceptance of gender alternatives is similar to that of other societies in Southeast Asia. There are also important differences, however, partly due to Indonesia's colonial and postcolonial history and to the contemporary importance of Islam. Also described in this chapter are the lives of some transgendered Indonesian males who have migrated to the Netherlands.

In chapter 7, I explore Euro-American gender diversity as it has changed historically—and in cycles—in the perceived relationship between sex/gender diversity and sexuality. Prior to the nineteenth century, multiple genders, rather than the binary oppositions of male and female, man and woman, and heterosexual and homosexual, dominated the sex/gender ideology. Within this context of historical change, I examine two variant female sex/gender roles, the "transvestite saint" and the "sworn virgin." I also consider the contemporary expansion of transgenderism as well as the importance of twentieth-century medical authority in affecting transsexualism and intersexuality.

The final chapter, chapter 8, "Variations on a Theme," summarizes some of the more important concepts discussed in the ethnographic chapters and reiterates some issues described in this introduction, including an expanded section on globalization.

ANTHROPOLOGY AND CULTURAL DIFFERENCE

Ethnographic descriptions of crosscultural variation of sex/gender diversity demonstrate the different meanings of this concept in different cultures. They raise our consciousness about the cultural construction of sex, gender, and sexualities and their relationship to each other in all societies. This emphasis on cultural difference foregrounds sex/gender ideologies that are practically unimaginable to people in different cultures. The focus on cultural difference also emphasizes that there is no one correct or superior way to organize sex/gender categories or to treat sex/gender nonconformity.

   If anthropology is about difference, however, it is also about bridging difference. In the classical anthropological tradition of looking at "other cultures" from the inside, and one's own culture from the outside, we are enabled to cross the barriers of cultural difference to a recognition of a greater shared humanity. This is the heart of cultural anthropology as a humanistic as well as a scientific discipline and one of my central purposes in writing this book.

Chapter One

Multiple Genders among Native Americans

The early encounters between Europeans and Native Americans in the fifteenth through the seventeenth centuries brought together cultures with very different sex/gender systems. The Spanish explorers, coming from a Catholic society where sodomy was a heinous crime, were filled with contempt and outrage when they recorded the presence of men in Native North American societies who performed the work of women, dressed like women, and had sexual relations with men (Lang 1996; Roscoe 1995).

Europeans labeled these men *berdache*, a term originally meaning male prostitute. The term was both insulting and inaccurate, derived from the European view that these roles centered on the "unnatural" and sinful practice of sodomy as defined in their own societies. This European ethnocentrism also caused early observers to overlook the specialized and spiritual functions of many of these roles and the positive value attached to them in many Native American societies.

By the late-nineteenth and early-twentieth centuries, some anthropologists included accounts of Native American sex/gender diversity in their ethnographies, attempting to explain the contributions alternative sex/gender roles made to social structure or culture. These accounts, though less contemptuous than earlier ones, nevertheless largely retained the ethnocentric emphasis on berdache sexuality, defining it as a form of "institutionalized homosexuality." Influenced by functionalist theory, anthropologists viewed these sex/gender roles as functional because they provided a social niche for male individuals whose personality and sexual orientation did not match the definition of masculinity in the anthropologists' societies, or because the roles

11

provided a "way out" of the masculine or warrior role for "cowardly" or "failed" men (see Callender and Kochems 1983).

Increasingly, however, anthropological accounts paid more attention to the association of Native American sex/gender diversity with shamanism and spiritual powers; they also noted that mixed gender roles were often central and highly valued, rather than marginal and deviant within some Native American societies. Still, the identification of Native American sex/gender diversity with European concepts of homosexuality (erotic feelings for a person of the same sex), transvestism (cross-dressing), or hermaphroditism (the presence of both male and female sexual organs in an individual) continued to distort their indigenous meanings.

In Native American societies, the European homosexual/heterosexual dichotomy was not culturally relevant as a central or defining aspect of gender. While mixed sex/gender individuals in many Native American societies did engage in sexual relations and even married persons of the same sex, this was not central to their alternative gender role. Europeans also overemphasized the function of cross-dressing in these roles, labeling such individuals as **transvestites** (**cross-dressers**); although mixed gender roles often did involve cross-dressing, this varied both within and among Native American societies. The label "hermaphrodite" was also inaccurate as a general category, although some societies did recognize biological intersexuality as the basis of sex/gender variation.

Given the great variation in Native North American societies, it is perhaps most useful to define their nonnormative sex/gender roles as referring to people who partly or completely adopted aspects of the culturally defined role of the other sex or gender and who were classified as neither woman nor man but as mixed, alternative genders; these roles did not involve a complete crossing over to an opposite sex/gender role (see Callender and Kochems 1983:443).

Both Native American sex/gender diversity and anthropological understandings of these roles have shifted in the past 30 years (Jacobs, Thomas, and Lang 1997: Introduction). Most current research rejects institutionalized homosexuality as an adequate explanation of Native American sex/gender diversity: It emphasizes occupation rather than sexuality as its central feature; considers multiple sex/gender roles as normal, indeed often integrated into and highly valued in Native American sex/gender systems (Albers 1989:134; Jacobs et al. 1997; Lang 1998); notes the variation in such roles across indigenous North (and South) America (Callender and Kochems 1983; Jacobs et al. 1997; Lang 1998; Roscoe 1998); and calls attention to the association of such roles with spiritual power (Roscoe 1996; Williams 1992).

Consistent with these new perspectives, the term "berdache" is somewhat out of fashion, though there is no unanimous agreement on what should replace it. One widely accepted suggestion is the term

Berdache, by Joe Lawrence Lembo, 1987. (Tempera on paper, 18 × 24.)

two-spirit (Jacobs et al. 1997; Lang 1998), a term coined in 1990 by urban Native American gays and lesbians. Two-spirit has the advantage of conveying the spiritual nature of gender variance in both traditional and contemporary Native American societies, although it emphasizes the Euro-American binary sex/gender construction of male and female/man and woman, which did not characterize all Native American groups.

DISTRIBUTION AND CHARACTERISTICS OF VARIANT SEX/GENDER ROLES

Multiple sex/gender systems were found in many, though not all, Native American societies. Variant male sex/gender roles are documented for 110 to 150 societies, occurring most frequently in the region extending from California to the Mississippi Valley and the upper-Great Lakes, the Plains and the Prairies, the Southwest, and to a lesser extent along the Northwest Coast. With few exceptions, gender variance is not historically documented for eastern North America, though it may have existed prior to the European invasion and disappeared before it could be recorded historically (Callender and Kochems 1983; Fulton and Anderson 1992).

There were many variations in Native American sex/gender diversity. Some cultures included three or four genders: men, women, male variants, and female variants (e.g., biological females who, by engaging in male activities, were reclassified as to gender). Gender variant roles also differed in the criteria by which they were defined; the degree of their integration into the society; the norms governing their behavior; the way the role was publicly acknowledged or sanctioned; how others were expected to behave toward gender variant persons; the degree to which a gender changer was expected to adopt the role of the opposite sex or was limited in doing so; the power, sacred or secular, that was attributed to them; and the path to recruitment.

In spite of this variety, however, there were also some widespread similarities: transvestism, cross-gender occupation, same-sex (but different gender) sexuality, a special process or ritual surrounding recruitment, special language and ritual roles, and associations with spiritual power.

TRANSVESTISM

Transvestism (***cross-dressing***) was often associated with gender variance but was not equally important in all societies. Male gender variants frequently adopted women's dress and hairstyles partially or completely, and female gender variants partially adopted the clothing of men; in some societies, however, transvestism was prohibited. The choice of clothing was sometimes an individual matter, and gender variants might mix their clothing and their accessories. For example, a female gender variant might wear a woman's dress but carry (male) weapons. Dress was also sometimes situationally determined: a male gender variant would have to wear men's clothing while engaging in warfare but might wear women's clothing at other times. Similarly, female gender variants might wear women's clothing when gathering (women's work) but male clothing when hunting (men's work) (Callender and Kochems 1983:447). Among the Navajo, a male gender variant, ***nádleeh***, would adopt almost all aspects of a woman's dress, work, language, and behavior; the Mohave male gender variant, called ***alyha***, was at the extreme end of the cross-gender continuum in imitating female physiology as well as transvestism. The repression and ultimately the almost total decline of transvestism was a direct result of US prohibitions against it.

OCCUPATION

The occupational aspects of Native American gender variance was central in most societies. Most frequently a boy's interest in the tools and activities of women and a girl's interest in the tools of male occupations signaled an individual's wish to undertake a gender variant role (Callender and Kochems 1983:447; Whitehead 1981). In hunting societies, for example, female gender variance was signaled by a girl rejecting the domestic activities associated with women and participating in playing and hunting with boys. In the Arctic and sub-Arctic this might be encouraged by a girl's parents if there were not enough boys to provide the family with food (Lang 1998). Male gender variants were frequently considered especially skilled and industrious in women's crafts and domestic work (though not in agriculture, where this was a man's task) (Roscoe 1991; 1996). Female gender crossers sometimes won the reputation of superior hunters and warriors.

The households of male gender variants were often more prosperous than others, sometimes because they were hired by whites. In their own societies the excellence of male gender variants' craftwork was sometimes ascribed to a supernatural sanction for their gender transformation (Callender and Kochems 1983:448). Female gender variants opted out of motherhood, so they were not encumbered by caring for children, which may explain their success as hunters or warriors. In some societies, gender variants could engage in both men's and women's work, and this, too, accounted for their increased wealth. Another source of income was payment for the special social activities due to gender variants' intermediate gender status, such as acting as go-betweens in marriage. Through their diverse occupations, then, gender variants were often central rather than marginal in their societies.

The explanation of male gender variant roles as a niche for "failed" or cowardly men who wished to avoid warfare or other aspects of the masculine role is no longer widely accepted. To begin with, masculinity was not associated with warrior status in all Native American cultures. In some societies, male gender variants were warriors, and in many others, males who rejected the warrior role did not become gender variants. Sometimes male gender variants did not go to war because of cultural prohibitions against their using symbols of maleness, for example, the prohibition against their using the bow among the Illinois. Where male gender variants did not fight, they sometimes had other important roles in warfare, like treating the wounded, carrying supplies for the war party, or directing postbattle ceremonials (Callender and Kochems 1983:449). In a few societies male gender variants became outstanding warriors, such as Finds Them and Kills Them, a

Crow Indian who performed daring feats of bravery while fighting with the United States Army against the Crow's traditional enemies, the Lakota Sioux (Roscoe 1998:23).

GENDER VARIANCE AND SEXUALITY

While generally sexuality was not central in defining gender status among Native Americans, in some Native American societies same-sex sexual desire or practices were significant in the definition of gender variant roles (Callender and Kochems 1983:449). Some early reports noted specifically that male gender variants lived with and/or had sexual relations with women as well as with men; in other societies they were reported as having sexual relations only with men, and in still other societies, of having no sexual relationships at all (Lang 1998:189–95).

The bisexual orientation of some gender variant persons may have been a culturally accepted expression of their gender variance. It may have resulted from an individual's life experiences, such as the age at which he or she entered the gender variant role, and/or it may have been one aspect of the general freedom of sexual expression in many Native American societies. While male and female gender variants most frequently had sexual relations with, or married, persons of the same biological sex as themselves, these relationships were not considered homosexual in the contemporary Western understanding of that term. In a multiple gender system the partners would be of the same sex but different genders, and homogender, rather than homosexual, practices bore the brunt of negative cultural sanctions (as is true today, for example, in contemporary Indonesia). The sexual partners of gender variants were never considered gender variants themselves.

Among the Navajo there were four genders; man, woman, and two gender variants: the masculine female-bodied nádleeh and the feminine male-bodied nádleeh (Thomas 1997). A sexual relationship between a female-bodied nádleeh and a woman or a sexual relationship between a male-bodied nádleeh and a man were not stigmatized because these persons were of different genders, although they were of the same biological sex. A sexual relationship between two women, two men, two female-bodied nádleeh, or two male-bodied nádleeh, however, was considered homosexual, and even incestual, and was strongly disapproved of.

The relation of sexuality to variant sex/gender roles across North America suggests that sexual relations between gender variants and per-

Opposite page: Finds Them and Kills Them, a Crow Indian gender variant, widely known as a superior warrior. (National Anthropological Archives, Smithsonian Institution, NAA IV 00476200.)

sons of the same biological sex were a result rather than a cause of gender variance. Sexual relationships between a man and a male gender variant were accepted in most Native American societies, though not in all, and appear to have been negatively sanctioned only when it interfered with child-producing heterosexual marriages. Gender variants' sexual relationships might be casual and wide-ranging (Europeans used the term "promiscuous"), or stable, and sometimes involved life-long marriages. In some societies, however, male gender variants were not permitted to engage in long-term relationships with men, either in or out of wedlock, and many male gender variants were reported as living alone.

A man might desire sexual relations with a (male) gender variant for different reasons: In some societies taboos on sexual relations with menstruating or pregnant women restricted opportunities for sexual intercourse; in other societies sexual relations with a gender variant person were exempt from punishment for extramarital affairs; in still other societies, for example among the Navajo, some gender variants were considered especially lucky, and a man might hope to have this luck transferred to himself though sexual relations (Lang 1998:349).

BIOLOGICAL SEX AND GENDER TRANSFORMATIONS

European observers often confused gender variants with **hermaphrodites** (biologically intersexed persons). Some Native American societies explicitly distinguished hermaphrodites from gender variants and treated them differently; others assigned gender variant persons and hermaphrodites to the same alternative gender status. In most Native American societies biological sex (or the intersexed condition of the hermaphrodite) was not the criterion for a gender variant role, nor were the individuals who occupied gender variant roles anatomically abnormal. The Navajo were an exception: They distinguished between the intersexed and the alternatively gendered but treated them similarly, though not exactly the same (Thomas 1997; Hill 1935).

Even as the traditional Navajo sex/gender system had biological sex as its starting point, the Navajo nádleeh were also distinguished by gender-linked behaviors, such as body language, clothing, ceremonial roles, speech style, and occupation. Feminine, male-bodied nádleeh might engage in women's activities such as cooking, weaving, household tasks, and making pottery. Masculine, female-bodied nádleeh, unlike other female-bodied persons, avoided childbirth; today they are associated with male occupational roles such as construction or firefighting (although ordinary women also sometimes engage in these occupations). Traditionally, female-bodied nádleeh had specific roles in Navajo ceremonials (Thomas 1997).

Thus, even where hermaphrodites occupied a special gender variant role, Native American gender variance was defined more by cultural than biological criteria. In the recorded case of a physical examination of a gender variant male, the previously mentioned Finds Them and Kills Them, his genitals were found to be completely normal (Roscoe 1998).

Native American gender variants were not generally conceptualized as hermaphrodites, but neither were they conceptualized as transsexuals (people who change from their original sex to the opposite sex). Gender transformations among gender variants were recognized as only a partial transformation, and the gender variant was not thought of as having become a person of the opposite sex/gender. Rather, gender variant roles were autonomous gender roles that combined the characteristics of men and women and had some unique features of their own. For example, among the Zuni a male gender variant was buried in women's dress but also in men's trousers on the men's side of the graveyard (Parsons, cited in Callender and Kochems 1983:454; Roscoe 1991:124, 145). Male gender variants were neither men—by virtue of their chosen occupations, dress, demeanor, and possibly sexuality—nor women, because of their anatomy and their inability to bear children. Only among the Mohave do we find the extreme imitation of women's physiological processes related to reproduction and the claims to have female sexual organs—both of which were ridiculed within Mohave society. Even here, however, where informants reported that female gender variants did not menstruate, this did not make them culturally men. Rather, it was the mixed quality of gender variant status that was culturally elaborated in Native North America and was the source of supernatural powers sometimes attributed to them.

SACRED POWER

The association between the spiritual power and gender variance occurred in most, if not all, Native American societies. Even where, as previously noted, recruitment to the role was occasioned by a child's interest in occupational activities of the opposite sex, supernatural sanction, frequently appearing in visions or dreams, was also involved, as among Prairie and Plains societies. These visions involved female supernatural figures, often the moon. Among the Omaha, the moon appeared in a dream holding a burden strap—a symbol of female work—in one hand, and a bow—a symbol of male work—in the other. When the male dreamer reached for the bow, the moon forced him to take the burden strap (Whitehead 1981). Among the Mohave, a child's choice of male or female implements heralding gender variant status was sometimes prefigured by a dream that was believed to come to an embryo in the womb (Devereux 1937).

In some but not all societies, sex/gender variants had sacred ritual roles and curing functions (Callender and Kochems 1983:453; Lang 1998). Where feminine qualities were associated with these roles, male gender variants might become spiritual leaders or healers, but where these roles were associated with masculine qualities they were not entered into by male gender variants. The Plains Indians, who emphasized a vision as a source of supernatural power, regarded male gender variants as holy persons, but California Indian societies did not. Moreover, in some Native American societies gender variants were specifically excluded from religious roles (Lang 1998:167). Nevertheless, sacred power was so widely associated with sex/gender diversity in Native North America that scholars generally agree that it is an important explanation of why such roles were so widespread.

In spite of cultural differences among Native American societies, some of their general characteristics are consistent with the positive value placed on sex/gender diversity and the widespread existence of multigender systems (Lang 1996). One cultural similarity is a cosmology (system of religious beliefs) in which transformation and ambiguity are recurring themes, applying to humans, animals, and objects in the natural environment. In many of these cultures, sex/gender ambiguity, lack of sexual differentiation, and sex/gender transformations are central in creation stories (Lang 1996:187). Native American cosmology may not be "the cause" of sex/gender diversity but it certainly (as in India) provides a hospitable context for it.

THE ALYHA: A MALE GENDER VARIANT ROLE AMONG THE MOHAVE

One of the most complete classic anthropological descriptions of a gender variant role in Native North America comes from the Mohave, who occupy the southwest desert area of the Nevada/California border. This description is based on interviews by anthropologist George Devereux (1937) with some aged informants who remembered the transvestite ceremony and had heard stories about gender variant individuals from their elders.

The Mohave had two gender variant roles: a male role called alyha and a female role called *hwame.* In this society, pregnant women had dreams forecasting the anatomic sex of their children. Mothers of a future alyha dreamt of male characteristics, such as arrow feathers, indicating the birth of a boy, but their dreams also included hints of their child's future gender variant status. A boy indicated he might become an alyha by "acting strangely" around the age of 10 or 11, before he had participated in the boys' puberty ceremonies. At this age, young people began to engage seriously in the activities that would character-ize their adult lives as men and women; boys learned to hunt, ride horses, and make bows and arrows; boys developed sexual feelings for girls. A potential alyha avoided these masculine activities. Instead he played with dolls, imitated the domestic work of women, tried to partic-ipate in the women's gambling games, and demanded to wear the female bark skirt rather than the male breechclout.

The alyha's parents and relatives were ambivalent about this behavior. His parents would initially try to dissuade him, but if the behavior persisted, his relatives would resign themselves and begin preparations for the transvestite ceremony. The ceremony was meant to take the boy by surprise; it was considered both a test of his inclina-tion and an initiation. Word was sent out to various settlements so that people could watch the ceremony and get accustomed to the boy in female clothing. At the ceremony, the boy was led into a circle of onlook-ers by two women as the crowd sang the transvestite songs. If the boy began to dance the women's dance, he was confirmed as an alyha. He was then taken to the river to bathe and given a girl's skirt to wear. This initiation ceremony confirmed his changed gender status, which was considered permanent.

After this ceremony the alyha assumed a female name (though he did not take the lineage name that all females assumed) and refused to answer to his former, male name. In the frequent and bawdy sexual jok-ing characteristic of Mohave culture, an alyha also resented male nomenclature being applied to his genitals. He insisted that his penis be called a clitoris, his testes, labia majora, and anus, a vagina. Alyha were particularly sensitive to sexual joking; if they were teased as women were, they assaulted those who teased them. Because alyha were very strong, people usually avoided angering them.

Alyha were considered highly industrious and much better house-wives than young girls. Therefore, they had no difficulty finding (male) spouses, and most alyha had husbands. Alyha were courted differently than ordinary girls. In conventional courtship the prospective husband would sleep chastely beside a girl for several nights and then lead her out of her parents' house, confirming the marriage; alyha in contrast, were courted like widows, divorcees, or "wanton" women. Intercourse with an alyha was surrounded by special etiquette. Like Mohave het-erosexual couples, the alyha and her husband practiced both anal and oral intercourse, with the alyha taking the female role. Alyha were reported to be embarrassed by an erection and would not allow their sexual partners to touch or even comment on their erect penises.

An alyha who found a husband would begin to imitate menstrua-tion by scratching herself between the legs with a stick until blood appeared. She then submitted to girls' puberty rites, and her husband also observed the requirements of a husband whose wife menstruated for the first time. Alyha also imitated pregnancy, particularly if their husbands threatened them with divorce on the grounds of barrenness. At this time they would cease faking menstruation and follow the pregnancy taboos, with even more attention than ordinary women, except that they publicly proclaimed their pregnancy, which ordinary Mohave women never did. To imitate pregnancy, an alyha would stuff rags in her skirts, and near the time of the birth she drank a decoction to cause constipation. After a day or two of stomach pains, she would go into the bushes and sit over a hole, defecating in the position of childbirth. The feces would be treated as a stillbirth and buried, and the alyha would weep and wail as a woman does for a stillborn child. The alyha and her husband would then clip their hair as in mourning.

Alyha were generally regarded as peaceful people, except when teased, and were also considered to be cowards. They did not participate in the frequent and harsh military raids of Mohave men and in the welcoming home feast for the warriors, as other old women did. Rather, alyha might make a bark penis and go through the crowd poking the men who had stayed home, saying, "You are not a man, but an alyha."

In general, alyha were not teased or ridiculed for being alyha (though their husbands were teased for marrying them), because it was believed it was their fate. The future alyha's desire for a gender change was such that he could not resist dancing the women's dance at the initiation ceremony, and once his desires were demonstrated in this manner, people would not thwart him. It was partly the belief that becoming an alyha was a result of a "temperamental compulsion" or was predestined (as forecast in his mother's pregnancy dream) that inhibited ordinary Mohave from ridiculing alyha. In addition, alyha were considered powerful healers, especially effective in curing sexually transmitted diseases (also called alyha) like syphilis.

Alyha illustrate one version of how sex/gender variant roles were constructed as autonomous genders in North America. In many ways the alyha crossed genders, but the role had a distinct, alternative status to that of both man and woman (as did the hwame). Although alyha imitated many aspects of a woman's role—dress, sexual behavior, menstruation, pregnancy, childbirth, and domestic occupations—they were also recognized as being different from women. Alyha did not take women's lineage names; they were not courted like ordinary women; they publicly proclaimed their pregnancies; and they were considered more industrious than other women in women's domestic tasks. In spite of alyha's sexual relations with men, alyha were not considered primarily homosexual (in Western terms). In fact, among ordinary Mohave, if a person dreamed of having homosexual relationships, that person would be expected to die soon, but this did not apply to alyha.

FEMALE GENDER VARIANTS

Female gender variants probably occurred more frequently among Native Americans than in other cultures, a point largely overlooked in the historic and ethnographic record (see Blackwood 1984; Jacobs et al. 1997; Lang 1998; Medicine 1983).

Although the generally egalitarian social structures of many Native American societies provided a hospitable context for female gender variance, it occurred in perhaps only one-quarter to one-half of the societies with male variant roles (Callender and Kochems 1983:446; see also Lang 1998:262–265). This may be explained partly by the fact that in many Native American societies women could—and did—adopt aspects of the male gender role, such as engaging in warfare or hunting, and sometimes dressed in male clothing, without being reclassified into a different gender (Blackwood 1984; Lang 1998:261ff; Medicine 1983).

As with males, the primary criterion of variant gender status for females was an affinity for the occupations of the other gender. While this inclination for male occupations was often displayed in childhood, female gender variants entered these roles later in life than did males (Lang 1998:303). Among some Inuit, "men pretenders" would refuse to learn women's tasks and their fathers taught them male occupations in childhood. They played with boys and participated in the hunt. Among the Kaska, a family who had only daughters might select one to "be like a man," as her hunting role could help provide the family with food. Among the Mohave, too, hwame refused to learn women's work, played with boys, and were considered excellent providers, as well as particularly efficient healers (Blackwood 1984:30; Lang 1998:286). Among the Cheyenne, the *hetaneman* (defined as a hermaphrodite having more of the female element) were great female warriors who accompanied the male warrior societies into battle. In all other groups, however, even outstanding women warriors were not recast into a different gender role (Roscoe 1998:75). Female gender variants also sometimes entered specialized occupations, becoming traders, guides for whites, or healers. The female preference for male occupations might be motivated by a female's desire to be independent, or it might be initiated or encouraged by a child's parents; in some societies it was sanctioned through supernatural omens or in dreams.

In addition to occupation, female gender variants might assume other characteristics of men. Cocopa *warrhameh* wore a masculine hairstyle and had their noses pierced, like boys (Lang 1998:283). Among the Maidu, the female *suku* also had her nose pierced on the occasion of her initiation into the men's secret society. Mohave hwame were tattooed like men instead of women. Transvestism was commonly though not universally practiced: it occurred, for example, among the Kaska, Paiute, Ute, and Mohave.

Like male gender variants, female gender variants exhibited a wide range of sexual relationships. Some had relationships with other females, who were generally regarded as ordinary women. Only rarely, as among a southern Apache group, was the female gender variant (like her male counterpart) defined in terms of her sexual desire for women. Mohave hwame engaged in sexual and marriage relationships with women, although they courted them in a special way, different from heterosexual courtships. If a hwame married a pregnant woman, she could claim paternity, although the child belonged to the descent group of its biological father (Devereux 1937:514). Like an alyha's husband, a hwame's wife was often teased and hwame marriages were generally unstable. The well-known hwame, Masahai Amatkwisai, married women three times and had sexual relationships with many men as well. Masahai's wives were all aggressively teased by male Mohave who viewed "real" sexual relations only in terms of penetration by a penis. At dances Masahai sat with the men, described her wife's genitals, and flirted with girls, all typical male behavior. Masahai's masculine behavior was ridiculed, and the men gravely insulted her (though never to her face), by referring to her by an obscene nickname meaning the female genitals. The harassment of Masahai's wives apparently led to the eventual breakup of her marriages.

Sexual relationships were generally downplayed in female gender variant roles, even when this involved marriage. One female gender variant, for example, Woman Chief, a famous Crow warrior and hunter, took four wives, but this appeared to be primarily an economic strategy: Processing animal hides among the Crow was women's work, so that Woman Chief's polygyny (multiple spouses) complemented her hunting skills.

While most often Native American women who crossed genders occupationally, such as Woman Chief, were not reclassified into a gender variant role, several isolated cases of female gender transformations have been documented historically. One of these is Ququnak Patke, a "manlike woman" from the Kutenai (Schaeffer 1965). Ququnak Patke had married a white fur trader, and when she returned to her tribe, she claimed that her husband had transformed her into a man. She wore men's clothes, lived as a man, married a woman, and claimed supernatural sanction for her role change and her supernatural powers. Although whites often mistook her for a man in her various roles as warrior, explorer's guide, and trader, such transformations were not considered a possibility among the Kutenai, and many thought Ququnak Patke was mad. She died attempting to mediate a quarrel between two hostile Indian groups.

Because sexual relations between women in Native American societies were rarely historically documented, it is hard to know how far we can generalize about the relation of sexuality to female gender variance in precontact Native American cultures. The few descriptions (and those for males, as well) are mainly based on ethnographic accounts that relied on twentieth-century informants whose memories were already shaped by white hostility toward gender diversity and same-sex sexuality. Nevertheless, it seems clear that although Native American female gender variants clearly had sexual relationships with women, sexual object choice was not their defining characteristic. In some cases, they were described "as women who never marry"; this does not say anything definitive about their sexuality and it may be that the sexuality of female gender variants was more variable than that of men.

As Masahai's and Ququnak Patke's stories illustrate, contact with whites opened up opportunities for gender divergent individuals, males as well as females (see Roscoe 1998; 1991). Overall, however, as a result of Euro-American repression and the growing assimilation of Euro-American sex/gender ideologies, Native American female and male gender variant roles largely disappeared by the 1930s, as the reservation system was well under way. Yet, their echoes may remain, both in the anthropological interest in this subject and in the activism of contemporary two-spirit individuals.

Review and Reflection

1. Describe three types of gender diverse roles in Native American societies and the criteria by which they were defined.

2. Discuss some of the functions of gender diversity for individuals and their families in different Native American societies.

3. Explain the role of sexuality in European perceptions of Native American gender diversity. Compare and contrast this perception with Native American understandings of sex/gender diversity.

4. Define the Mohave alyha. List five alyha attributes, including, for example, conditions of birth, expected behavior, ritual elements, and others that define the alyha in Mohave society.

5. Relate the role of religion to gender diversity among Native Americans, using examples from the chapter. (Looking ahead: Compare and contrast this to the relation of religion to gender diversity in Brazil.)

6. Summarize three examples of female gender diverse roles in different Native American societies and compare them with three male roles in terms of criteria and functions.

Chapter Two

Hijra and Sādhin
Neither Man nor Woman
in India and Bangladesh

Jazlyn

Sex/gender diversity in Hindu India is mainly set within a religious context. **Hijras** are constructed as a third gender, neither man nor woman, and both man and woman, within a basically binary, hierarchical, and patriarchal sex/gender system; male and female/man and woman are viewed as natural categories in complementary opposition. This binary construction incorporates—and conflates—biological qualities (sex) and cultural qualities (gender). Males and females are born with different sexual characteristics and reproductive organs, have different sexual natures, and take different and complementary roles in marriage, sexual behavior, and reproduction. This biological nature of sex/gender differences is described in classical Hindu medical and ritual texts, in which body fluids and sexual organs are presented as both the major sources of the sex/gender dichotomy and its major symbols (O'Flaherty 1980).

In Hinduism, in contrast to Western culture, it is the more active female principle that animates the more inert and latent male principle. This active female principle has an erotic, creative, life-giving aspect and a destructive, life-destroying aspect. The erotic aspect of female power is dangerous unless it is controlled by the male principle. Powerful women, whether deities or humans, must be restrained by male authority. In both Hinduism and Islam, women are believed to be more sexually voracious than men; in order to prevent their sexual appetites from causing social chaos women must be controlled.

27

GENDER DIVERSITY IN HINDUISM

Indian sex/gender diversity is mainly associated with Hinduism, though hijras also have important connections to Islam (Nanda 1999; Reddy 2005; Hossain 2012a). In spite of its emphasis on the basic complementary opposition of male and female, Hinduism acknowledges many sex/gender variants and transformations. In contrast to Western religions, which try to resolve, repress, or trivialize sexual contradictions and ambiguities, Hinduism "celebrates the idea that the universe is boundlessly various, and . . . that all possibilities may exist without excluding each other" (O'Flaherty 1973:318). This view gives positive meaning to the lives of individuals with a variety of alternative gender identifications, physical conditions, and erotic preferences. Despite the criminalization of sodomy under British rule and even after independence, Indian society is not characterized by culturally institutionalized phobias and repressions regarding alternative sex/gender roles.

Ancient Hindu origin myths feature androgynous or hermaphroditic ancestors. Multiple sexes and genders are acknowledged, although sometimes ambivalently, as possibilities among both humans and deities. The classic Hindu religious text, the Ṛg Veda, for example, says that before creation the world lacked all distinctions, including those of sex and gender. Ancient poets often expressed this concept with androgynous or hermaphroditic images, such as a male with a womb, a male deity with breasts, or a pregnant male (Zwilling and Sweet 2000:101). While sex/gender variation may be stigmatized, individuals in nonnormative sex/gender roles may also find, within Hinduism, meaningful and valued gender identifications.

This Hindu "propensity towards androgynous thinking" underlies the interchange of male and female qualities, transformations of sex and gender, the incorporation of male and female within one person, and alternative sex and gender roles among deities and humans as meaningful and positive themes in Hindu mythology, ritual, and art. Hijras are the most visible and culturally institutionalized sex/gender variants in India.

Hijras, culturally defined as "neither man nor woman," are sexually impotent males who undergo removal of their male genitals to achieve the ritual power that Hinduism attributes to sexual renunciation (Nanda 1999). Hijras worship Bahuchara Mata, a form of the Hindu Mother Goddess particularly associated with transgenderism. Their traditional employment is as musical entertainers at marriages and at the birth of a (male) child, during which they bless the bridal couple and child for fertility and prosperity in the name of the goddess. In return they receive traditional payments of money, sweets, and cloth.

HIJRAS AS NOT-MEN . . .

As early as the eighth century BCE, Hinduism recognized alternative sex/gendered persons, who were primarily sexually impotent
males, unable to procreate (Zwilling and Sweet 1996:361), a concept
central to the contemporary English translation of hijra as "eunuch" or
"hermaphrodite." But hijras also adopt the clothing, behavior, and occupations of women. Thus, hijras are recognized, by themselves and others, as neither man nor woman but also as "both man and woman."

Hijra sexual impotence, popularly understood as a *physical* defect
impairing the male sexual function in intercourse (in the inserter role)
and in reproduction is the major way in which hijras are "not-men." In
fact, few hijras are born with defective genitals and not all individuals
"born that way" become hijras. Rather, this explanation of their deficient masculinity expresses the Hindu view that sex and gender are
biologically based and that fate is important in shaping one's life
chances and experiences.

Hijras frequently have sexual relationships with "normal" men;
while they often define themselves as "men who have no desire for
women," they are linguistically and culturally distinguished from
males who take the receptor role in sex and who are identified by their
same-sex sexual orientation but are not considered gender nonconformists (Cohen 1995; Reddy 2005, 2010).

Mirna

HIJRAS AS WOMEN AND NOT-WOMEN

While hijras are "man minus man," they are also "man plus
woman." Hijras wear women's clothing and accessories; wear their hair
long like women; and imitate women's walk, gestures, voice, facial
expressions, and language. Like the *waria* of Indonesia, hijras seek
only "normal" male sexual partners and positively experience themselves as objects of men's sexual desires. Males who become hijras take
feminine names and use female kinship terms within the hijra community, such as sister, aunty, and grandmother (Hall 1995). They request
"ladies only" seating on public transportation and periodically demand
to be counted as women, not men, in the census. Thus, being a hijra
requires both divesting oneself of one's masculine identity and also taking on a feminine one.

Although hijras are "like" women, they are also "not-women." Like
the Indonesian waria, their feminine dress and manners are often
exaggerations, and their aggressive female sexuality contrasts strongly

with the normatively submissive demeanor of ordinary women. Hijra performances are a burlesque: The very act of dancing in public violates Indian norms of feminine behavior. Also contrary to ideal feminine norms, hijras use coarse, abusive, and insulting speech in public. This was noted by early European observers and elicits comment in contemporary Indian media (Hall 1997).

As "neither man nor woman" hijras were sometimes prohibited from wearing women's clothing exclusively; some eighteenth-century Indian kings required hijras to distinguish themselves by wearing a man's turban with their female attire. In the nineteenth century hijras were reported as wearing "a medley of male and female clothing," with a female sari under a male, coat-like outer garment (Preston 1987:373); today most hijras do not wear gender-mixed clothing.

The major reason hijras are "not-woman" is because they cannot give birth. One hijra told me a story of a hijra who prayed to God to make it possible for her to have a child. God granted her wish and she became pregnant, but since she had not specifically prayed for the child to be born, she could not give birth. She remained pregnant until she could not stand the weight so she slit her stomach open to deliver the baby. Both the hijra and the baby died. My narrator viewed this story as a message that hijras are not complete women.

Chris

RELIGIOUS IDENTIFICATIONS

Hijras identify with Arjun, hero of the Hindu epic, the *Mahabharata*. In one episode Arjun is exiled and lives for a year in the disguise of a eunuch-transvestite, wearing women's dress and bracelets, braiding his hair like a woman, and teaching singing and dancing to the women of the king's court. In this role he also participates in weddings and childbirths, a clear point of identification with the hijras (Hiltelbeitel 1980). This identification is visually reinforced by Arjun's representation in sculptures and popular drama as a vertically divided half-man/half-woman. In this form, Arjun and hijras are also identified with the sexually ambivalent deity, Shiva, whose female aspect symbolizes his union with female energy.

Shiva is associated with the Hindu concept of *creative asceticism*, the core of hijra identity and power. In Hinduism, sexual impotence can be transformed into procreative power through the practice of asceticism, or the renunciation of sex. The power that results from sexual abstinence paradoxically becomes an essential feature in the process of creation. In one Hindu creation myth Shiva was asked to create the world but delayed so long that the power of creation was given to another deity, Brahma (The Creator). When Shiva was finally ready to begin creation he saw that the universe was already created. He got so angry he broke off his phallus saying, "There is no use for this," and threw it into the earth, where it became a source of universal fertility (O'Flaherty 1973). This paradox is central to the power of the hijras who, as emasculated men, have the power to confer fertility on others. The auspiciousness and power of hijras as creative ascetics underlie their ritual performances at marriages and childbirth.

Asceticism offers an important alternative to normative gender roles in Hindu India, which are essentially related to marriage, having children, especially sons, and sustaining the family over generations. An individual who dies without being married, an impotent man, or a woman who does not menstruate is considered an incomplete person. By taking on the role of the ascetic, however, a person who renounces sexual desire, abandons his or her family, and depends on alms for livelihood can transform incomplete personhood into a transcendent one, and thereby achieve salvation.

Hijras' powers are also derived from their identification with a Hindu Mother Goddess, Bahuchara Mata. Popular Hindu mythology abounds in images of an aggressive and dangerous Mother Goddess, whose destructive acts contain the possibility of rebirth. Bahuchara Mata is particularly associated with male transvestism and transgenderism; several hijras are always present at her temple, near Ahmedabad, in Gujerat, to bless visitors and tell them about her powers.

Thus, hijras are not merely deficient males but are males who receive a call from their goddess—which they ignore at the peril of being born impotent for seven future rebirths—to undergo a change in sex and gender presentation; this involves an emasculation "operation" in which the testicles and penis are removed. Only after emasculation do hijras become vehicles of the procreative power of Bahuchara Mata. For hijras not born intersexed (and few are), the operation transforms an impotent, "useless" male into a hijra, whose powers regarding procreation are the cause of both the respect and the fear they engender in society.

During the emasculation surgery, ideally performed by a hijra "midwife," the client sits facing a picture of the goddess, repeating her name until the client falls into a trancelike state. The midwife then severs the penis and testicles from the body with two diagonal cuts from a sharp knife. The blood from the operation, considered part of the male identity, flows freely from the body, ridding the person of his maleness. After the operation the individual is considered "reborn," and the healing period incorporates the rituals surrounding childbirth. When healing is completed, the hijra is dressed as a bride, signifying the active sexuality potential in marriage, and is paraded through the streets, completing the sex/gender transformation.

Bahuchara Mata, a version of the Mother Goddess, is the special object of devotion for hijras. (Photograph by Serena Nanda.)

Chris

SOCIAL RESPONSES TO HIJRAS

Hijras are ambivalently welcomed at marriages and after the birth of a child, where their performances center on blessings for fertility. These performances contain flamboyant sexual displays and references to sexuality, which break all the rules of normal social intercourse in gender-mixed company and are a source of humor. The hijras' skits and songs refer to potentially conflicting relationships in Indian marriages, for example between mother-in-law and daughter-in-law, or between sisters-in-law (Nanda and Gregg 2009). As outsiders to the social structure because of their ambiguous sex/gender status, hijras are uniquely able to expose the points of tension in a culture where sex, gender, and reproduction are central and diffuse the tension through laughter.

The public regards hijras with a combination of mockery, fear, respect, contempt, and even compassion. Fear of hijras is related to the "virility complex" in Indian culture, which identifies manhood with semen and sexual potency, both of central concern in India's patriarchal society. Hijras have the power to curse as well as to bless; if they are not paid their due, they will curse a family with a loss of virility. The ultimate weapon of a hijra is to raise her skirt and display her mutilated genitals; this is both a source of shame and a contamination of the family's reproductive potential.

Hijras are also feared because they are outside the social roles and relationships of caste and kinship, which are the main sources of social control over an individual (Ostor, Fruzzetti, and Barnett 1982). Hijras, like other ascetics, are thus an implicit threat to the social order at the same time that they reinforce its most important values (Lannoy 1975; O'Flaherty 1973). Hijras use their sexual and social marginality to manipulate and exploit the public to their own economic advantage; they sometimes refer to themselves as a people without "shame" (Hall 1995; 1997:445). Hijra audiences feel vulnerable to this economic extor-

As part of their traditional ritual performance role when a son is born, hijras examine the baby's genitals to confirm his sex. (Photograph by Serena Nanda.)

tion and weigh the financial cost of giving in to the hijras' coercive demands for payment against the public abuse, humiliation, and curses that will be heaped on them if they refuse.

If hijras challenge their audiences, their audiences may also challenge hijras. Sometimes a spectator will challenge a hijra performer's authenticity by lifting her skirts to confirm that she is a "real," emasculated hijra, and not a "fake" hijra, that is, a man with male genitals who is only impersonating a hijra. A hijra found to be fake is insulted and chased away without payment.

HIJRA SEXUALITY

The term "hijra" does not mean "homosexual" in the Western sense of an identity based on same-sex sexual desire. Hijras do, however, widely engage in sexual activities, exclusively in the receptor role with men, and frequently as prostitutes, an "open secret" among urban working-class males. In large, cosmopolitan cities, such as Mumbai, hijra prostitutes may work out of brothels located in "red light" districts; in smaller locales they may use their own homes to carry on prostitution discretely.

In addition to prostitution, hijras, like the Indonesian waria, also have long-term sexual relationships with men they call their "husbands." These relationships may be one-sided and exploitative, as when the "husband" lives off his hijra "wife," but they may also be affectionate and involve some economic reciprocity. Most hijras prefer having a husband (or boyfriend) to engaging in prostitution and speak of their husbands in loving terms, as indeed some husbands speak of their hijra wives (Reddy 2006; Nanda 2010). For many hijras, joining the hijra community provides an opportunity to engage in sexual relations with men in a safer, more organized and orderly environment than is afforded by street prostitution.

Hijra sexual relationships, particularly prostitution, undermine the respect given to hijras based on their cultural definition as powerful ascetics; partly for this reason, hijra prostitutes may not be permitted to live with hijra ritual performers. Hijra elders are also often jealous of the attachment of individual hijras to their husbands, which undercuts the economic contribution of a hijra to her household. Some hijras complain that prostitution has increased because the opportunities for their ritual performances have declined. In fact, hijras have been known as prostitutes for hundreds of years, an association most hijras vehemently deny and attribute to those males who imitate their effeminacy but who are not "real" hijras. Hijras' sexual engagement as

In spite of their ideal role as ascetics, many hijras have long-term relationships with men whom they call their husbands. (Photograph by Serena Nanda.)

receptors of sexual penetration by "normal" men emphasizes their cultural construction as "failed" men, though as noted above, they are also culturally constructed as both man and woman.

SOCIAL STRUCTURE OF THE HIJRA COMMUNITY

Indian social structure is dominated by a caste system, in which distinct corporate social units are associated with occupational exclusivity, control over their members, and a hierarchically based group allocation of rights and privileges. Many different kinds of groups, such as Muslims and tribal peoples, originally outside the Hindu caste system, have been incorporated into it as caste-like groups. Hijra communities are highly organized and have many caste-like features, as well as local, regional, and national kinship networks, which contribute to their social reproduction (Nanda 1999). Like a caste, the hijra community claims a monopoly over its occupation as ritual performers; exercises control over its members, with outcasting as the ultimate sanction; and rests its legitimacy on origin myths associated with high-status legendary figures like Arjun or deities like Ram (embodying adherence to duty, virtue, and righteousness, as narrated in the Hindu epic, the *Ramayana*) or Shiva.

The Indian census does not count hijras separately, so estimates of their numbers are unreliable; a common "guesstimate" is 50,000 nationwide. Hijras are mainly associated with North Indian culture and mostly live in cities, which offer them the greatest opportunity to perform their traditional ritual roles. Small groups of hijras are found all over India, however, in the south as well as the north, in rural areas and small towns as well as in big cities, and, as we see below, in Pakistan and Bangladesh, formerly part of British India.

Hijras normally live in households containing between five and 20 members, managed by a hijra elder. Each hijra contributes to the running of the household, either with money or by performing domestic tasks. Household composition is flexible and individuals commonly move from one household to another in a different part of a city or in a different city or region, out of boredom, dissatisfaction, or as the result of a dispute.

The nationwide hijra community is composed of "houses," or named subgroups, which are not domestic units but function like lineages. Each house recognizes a common "ancestor" and has its own history and special rules. Any particular household contains members of several houses. Each house (not household) has a leader, or *naik* (chief), and within the major cities, the naiks of the different houses form a kind of executive council, making policy and resolving disputes.

Below the level of naik is the *guru* (master, teacher). The most significant relationship among hijras is that of guru and *chela* (disciple). An individual is formally initiated into the hijra community under the sponsorship of a guru, who bestows a new, female name on the chela and pays the initiation fee. The new chela vows to obey her guru and the rules of the house and the community; the guru presents the new chela with some gifts and records her name in the guru's record book. This guru–chela relationship, which replicates the ideals of an extended family, is ideally a lifelong bond of reciprocity: The guru is obligated to "take care of" the chela in return for the chela's loyalty, obedience, and a fixed percentage of her income.

Through the extension of guru–chela relationships, hijras all over India are related by (fictive) kinship (Hall 1995). "Daughters" of one "mother" consider themselves "sisters," and elders are regarded as "grandmothers" or as "mother's sister" (aunt). These relationships involve warm and reciprocal regard and are sometimes formalized by the exchange of small amounts of money, clothing, jewelry, and sweets. In addition to the constant movement of hijras who visit their gurus and fictive kin in different cities, religious and secular annual gatherings also bring together thousands of hijras from all over India.

Hijras come from Hindu, Muslim, or Christian families, and most seem to be from the lower, though not unclean (formerly, untouchable), castes. Within the hijra community, however, as with other ascetics, former caste affiliations are disregarded, though other signs of status, such as good looks, talent, and the ability to earn money are important. Whatever their religious background, Indian hijras identify to various degrees with Islam, partly because of the prestigious role of eunuchs in the Mughal courts, during the sixteenth–mid-nineteenth centuries, and partly because of the egalitarian structure of Islam, which ideally disregards differences of caste status (Reddy 2005).

In preindependent India, the caste-like status of the hijras was recognized in some princely states, which granted hijras hereditary rights to a parcel of land and the collection of food and alms from each agricultural household in a stipulated area. These rights were inherited within each hijra community, consistent with the Indian political concept of the king's duty to ensure the ancient rights of his subjects (Preston 1987:380). In British India, however, these rights were rejected, in an effort to discourage activities that "breach[ed] the laws of public decency" (Preston 1987:382). The British also enacted laws criminalizing emasculation, aimed specifically at the hijras; these laws were later incorporated into the criminal code of independent India, although emasculation continues to be practiced secretly (Ranade 1983). Sensationalized cases of (forced) emasculation are occasionally reported in the media and undermine public acceptance of hijras, as does the popular association of hijras with HIV/AIDS, though in fact, the spread of AIDS in India is primarily through heterosexual prostitution.

In addition, partly as a result of the increasing Westernization of Indian culture, the role of many traditional ritual performers like hijras is becoming less compelling. In an attempt to compensate for lost earnings, hijras have branched out occupationally: They now bless female as well as male children, perform at college functions, bless the opening of public buildings or new businesses, and act as tax collectors. Such are the adaptive possibilities in a culture where, despite great ambivalence, the alternative sex/gender role of hijras continues to find a place in a society where religion still gives positive meaning to gender variance and even accords it a measure of power.

Brian P

THE SĀDHIN: A FEMALE GENDER VARIANT

Female gender variants are mentioned in ancient Hindu texts, but are not as widespread, visible, or prominent as the hijras. The *sādhin* or female ascetic is a role that has become meaningful within the context of Hindu values and culture, particularly regarding the position of women in India (see Humes 1996) and the concept of the ascetic.

As noted above, marriage and reproduction are essential to recognition as a socially accepted person in Hindu India, and "spinsters" rarely exist in rural areas. Among the Gaddis, a numerically small pastoral people of the Himalayan foothills, the role of the sādhin emerged in the late-nineteenth century. Sādhins renounce marriage and thus, sexuality—they are committed to lifelong celibacy—though they otherwise live in the ordinary world. Sādhins wear the everyday clothing of men, not women, and wear their hair close cropped (Phillimore 1991).

A girl usually makes a voluntary decision to become a sādhin at the time she reaches puberty, but before her menarche (first menstrual cycle), though in one reported case, the parents of a six-year-old girl interpreted her preference to dress in boys' clothing and cut her hair like a boy as an indication of her choice to be a sādhin. For most sādhins, this role choice, which is considered irreversible, is related to their determined rejection of marriage. A sādhin must be a virgin; she is viewed, however, not just as a celibate woman but as an asexual female. Although the transition from presexual child to asexual sādhin denies a girl's sexual identity, the girl is not considered to have changed her gender, so much as transcended it.

Entering the sādhin role is not marked by ritual, but it is publicly acknowledged when the sādhin adopts men's clothing and has her hair cut in a tonsure, like a boy for his initiation rite into adulthood. Despite her male appearance, however, a sādhin remains socially a woman in many ways, and she retains the female name given to her when she was a child. Sādhins may (but are not obliged to) engage in masculine productive tasks from which women are normally excluded, for example, ploughing, sowing crops, sheep herding, and processing wool. They also, however, do women's work. On gender-segregated ceremonial occasions, adult sādhins may sit with the men as well as smoke the water pipe and cigarettes, definitely masculine behaviors. Yet, sādhins do not generally attend funerals, a specifically male prerogative.

Ethnographer Peter Phillimore characterizes the role of the sādhin as an "as if" male (1991:337). A sādhin's gender is not in question, but she can nevertheless operate in many social contexts "like a man." A sādhin can, for example, make the necessary offerings for her father's spirit and the ancestors, a ceremony otherwise performed only by a son. Unlike hijras, though, sādhins have no special ritual or performance roles in society, nor are they considered to have any special sacred powers. Sādhins, like hijras, are ascetics in their renunciation of sexuality, although sādhins are only ambiguous ascetics because they do not renounce other aspects of the material world.

Hindu asceticism is primarily identified with males so that female ascetics behave in significant respects like men; this maleness makes visible and legitimates female asceticism, though it is different from male asceticism in important ways (Humes 1996; Phillimore 1991:341). Unlike male ascetics, who transcend sex/gender classification and who can renounce the world at any age or stage of life, the sādhin's asceticism must begin before puberty and her lifelong chastity, or purity, is essential to the public acceptance of her status. These differences suggest that within orthodox Hinduism, the sādhin role is a way of controlling female sexuality and providing a social niche for the woman who rejects the only legitimate female roles in traditional Hindu India, those of wife and mother.

Because of the importance of women in the subsistence economy, Gaddi society was substantially more gender egalitarian than orthodox Hindus. When Gaddi migration in the late-nineteenth century brought them into contact with more orthodox Hindus, Gaddis came under increasing cultural pressure to curtail the relative equality and freedom of their women. However, because a woman's decision to reject marriage is an unacceptable challenge to gender conventions among the orthodox Hindus, the sādhin role functions as a constraint on the potential, unacceptable, sexuality of unmarried women. The definition of the sādhin as asexual transforms "the negative associations of spinsterhood" into the "positive associations of sādhin-hood" (Phillimore 1991:347).

The sādhin role provides one kind of response to the cultural challenge of adult female virginity in a society where marriage and motherhood are the dominant feminine ideals, while the hijra role, despite its many contradictions, gives meaning and even power to male sex/gender ambiguity in a highly patriarchal culture. While all cultures must deal with individuals whose anatomy or behavior leaves them outside the classification of male and female, man and woman, it is the genius of Hinduism that allows for so many different ways of being human.

THE HIJRAS OF BANGLADESH

Hijras also have a cultural role in Pakistan (Rais 1993; Pfeffer 1995) and Bangladesh, both Muslim majority regions in British India and now independent nations. Anthropologist Adnan Hossain's (2012a; 2012b) ethnographic research on hijras in Dhaka, the capital of Bangladesh, contributes new and important perspectives on hijra identity and broadens the contexts within which nonnormative sex/gender roles in South Asia need to be understood.

While Hossain notes both similarities and differences between Indian and Bangladeshi hijras, his in-depth ethnography is particularly useful in exploring the relationship of hijras to Islam and in emphasizing the erotic desire for "normal" men as a defining element in hijra lives and identities. This leads Hossain to define hijras as "feminine-identified male-bodied people who desire 'macho' men"; a definition that emphasizes hijra sexuality rather than gender ambiguity as central to their lives.

Among the many shared cultural and social features of Indian and Bangladeshi hijras are the importance of the guru–chela relationship, their belonging to organized "houses," the maintenance of recognized spatial boundaries within which they work, origin stories recognizing a Mother Goddess, and the low status accorded to their involvement in prostitution, an important source of income. Bangladeshi hijras also perform blessings at weddings and childbirths, although this work does not have the ritual significance it has in India.

A major contribution of Hossain's ethnography is to demonstrate the importance of hijras' sexual desire in the construction of their role in India and Bangladesh, both within and beyond their own community. Thus, although his definition of hijras does refer to them as "males who sacrifice their male genitals to a goddess in return for spiritual power," he also challenges the importance of emasculation in defining hijra authenticity both within the hijra community and for the public. Hossain also notes that while Bangladeshi hijras may be recognized as ascetics who renounce sexual desire, this is not taken seriously; it is hijras' erotic desires and sexual relations, rather than emasculation and renunciation, that is central to their identity.

While sexual relations with (normal) men, in which hijras act as recipients of male penetration, is also an important part of hijra life in India, in Bangladesh it is not merely a reality—the definition of its pleasures is, according to Hossain, central to how hijras see themselves. Indeed, Hossain defines the sexual desire to receive anal penetration by men as the motivation for why a person becomes a hijra (2012b:9). While this motivation is sometimes expressed by Indian hijras, it is intensely rejected by others. In addition, although the Indian hijra assertion that they were "born that way," (i.e., as males with physically undeveloped genitals) also finds expression in Bangladesh, this is inaccurate (as it is in India), though in Bangladesh it evokes a certain pity and includes hijras among the disabled, which mitigates public hostility.

Hossain notes that in Dhaka, in contrast to India, emasculated and nonemasculated hijras are accorded equal status. He also notes that in Dhaka there are hijras who are heteronormatively married and who play the normative masculine role in their families (which I did not come across in India), as well as hijras who exclusively identify with the feminine.

In contrast to the importance of emasculation to hijra authenticity in India, Hossain emphasizes that in Bangladesh it is the skills central to hijra engagement with the public, in both sexual and ritual encounters, that confer a status of authenticity. In addition to performance skills, it is the "magical" hijra ability to conceal one's penis, taught by gurus to hijras who are not emasculated, that is considered central to Bangladeshi hijra identity and is more important than emasculation (Hossain 2012b:497, 501, 506). In my fieldwork this "skill," which was not referred to as "magical," was described to me by a hijra prostitute, bragging about how she "fooled" men into thinking she was a woman by her ability to conceal her penis between her thighs (Nanda 1999:64). Hossain's demonstration of the importance of sexual desire in hijra lives not only provides an important alternative to the view of hijras as a third gender, but it also sheds light on concepts of masculinity in Bangladesh, an example of how the cultural margins can illuminate core cultural patterns.

Another important contribution of Hossain's ethnography is a detailed description of hijra relationships to Islam, a complicated issue (see also Gayatri Reddy [2005], a study of hijras in Hyderabad, India). Although, as in India, Bangladeshi hijras claim devotion to a Hindu Mother Goddess, acknowledge important Hindu-based origin stories, and sustain social ties with hijras in India, whom they visit, Bangladeshi hijras consider themselves Muslim, both through their commitments to Muslim religious beliefs and practices and their participation in Muslim rituals.

Bangladeshi hijras are devotees of Muslim saints and actively participate in several Muslim (Shi'ite) rituals. Some Bangladeshi hijras report that devout Muslims, including imams (religious leaders), even proselytize among them to encourage orthodox Muslim practice, such as the obligatory five daily prayers, but do not attempt to persuade them to forgo cross-dressing. In fact, some hijras themselves preach Islam to the wider public and even perform the hajj (pilgrimage to Mecca). While some Muslim shrines in Dhaka insist that hijras wear only masculine dress when they come to worship, hijras also visit some Muslim shrines dressed as women. As in Indonesia, then, the relation of the Bangladeshi hijras to Islam demonstrates Islam's historic syncretic and flexible nature.

In-depth personal narratives as well as Hossain's analysis demonstrate several major themes of this book: sex/gender diversity varies among individuals; it must be examined in relationship to many cultural, religious, social, and political factors; and individual identity and behavior, in both normative and nonnormative sex/gender roles, is not static. As noted in other cultures, identity is part of a lifetime process of "becoming" and changes in relation to local, national, and global contexts.

Review and Reflection

1. Analyze the role of Hinduism as it affects sex/gender diversity in India.
2. Describe the main characteristics of Indian hijras, including their social organization and at least two of their roles in society.

3. Explain creative asceticism and how it relates to the cultural definition of the hijras in India.

4. Illustrate, through examples of hijra behavior, how the ideal definition of "hijra" may diverge from the reality.

5. Summarize the role of the sādhin in India and explain the major ways it is different from the hijra role.

6. Explain, according to ethnographer Adnan Hossain, what are the major ways in which the hijras of Bangladesh are both similar to and different from, the hijras of India.

7. Discuss Islam in relation to the hijras of Bangladesh. (Looking ahead: Compare this with the relation of Islam to gender diversity in Indonesia.)

Chapter Three

Men and Not-Men
Sexuality and Gender in Brazil

In Brazil sex/gender diversity is associated with the alternative sex/gender roles of **travestí**, **viado**, and **bicha**, most centrally defined by their sexuality, a theme that characterizes most of Latin America (Murray 1995). Underlying cultural variations in the sex/gender ideologies of Latin America is a shared understanding, based on common roots in Spanish and Portuguese culture, of men and women as totally opposed in every way, with males clearly superior (Brandes 1981; Gilmore 1996). This pattern has been central throughout Brazilian history, though today it is one of several sex/gender ideologies that coexist in contradictory, complex, and overlapping ways in Brazil.

Brazil's traditional sex/gender system flowered in the early colonial period (sixteenth century) when a plantation slave economy dominated by a class of wealthy landowners was the predominant economic and cultural feature. Plantation landowner patriarchs exercised absolute authority over their dominions, resulting in a rigid social hierarchy of master over (African) slave and men over women. This intersecting class/race/gender hierarchy was sanctioned by official Catholic Church teachings and enforced, when necessary, through violence. Thus, the association of power, domination, and the use or threat of violence became central to Brazilian masculine identity and its system of sexual classification (Parker 1991:31). This traditional sex/gender ideology dominated Brazil throughout the nineteenth and early-twentieth centuries and still retains much of its power today.

The foundation of this system is the dichotomy between man and woman (or rather, as discussed later in this chapter, between man and not-man), masculine and feminine, which are opposed in every way.

43

This opposition is viewed as a natural result of the biological sex differences between males and females. It encompasses many differences—bodies and genitalia, social position, rights and responsibilities, psychological characteristics, sexual desires and capacities, and appropriate spatial and social domains. Men dominate the more important public spheres of political activity and the workplace, while women are acknowledged as superior only in realms regarded as inferior, such as domestic life (Hayes 1996:9).

Power is invested entirely in the hands of men, who are characterized by their superiority, strength, virility, activity, potential for violence, and legitimate use of force. Masculine virility is manifested in aggressive sexuality and having many children, and also by the ability to control the sexuality of women, that is, daughters and wives.

Women are defined as inferior and weak, yet also beautiful and desirable, and subject always to control by men—fathers and brothers and, after marriage, husbands. A persistent underlying threat to masculinity is the loss of control over women. Inherent in the beauty and seductiveness of women is the constant threat of their sexual betrayal, a view that has deep roots in the Christian ideology of women as either virgins, mothers, or whores (Gregg 1997; Parker 1991:49). Virginity is a sign of a woman's innocence and, more important, a demonstration of her proper domination by male authority. Both the prostitute and the unfaithful wife are a deeply felt threat to the system because each in her own way escapes the control of legitimate male authority (Hayes 1996:22). Any betrayal of male control is an insult to male honor; given the constant threat of betrayal, demonstrations of masculinity through a virile sexuality form an essential element in competitive displays between men (Gilmore 1996). The marked differentiation of the sexes justifies a double standard of morality. Men are given the freedom of carnal love independent of reproduction, while for women, sexual relations are joined to the obligation to conceive, give birth, and raise children within marriage.

Unlike the northern version of modern Euro-American culture, in which biological sex is the basis of gender classification crosscut by the homosexual/heterosexual dichotomy, in Brazil, the core gender opposition is based on sexuality, that is, the position taken in sexual intercourse. Brazilian gender ideology is based on the distinction between those who penetrate—the active (*atividade*), defined as masculine—and those who are penetrated—the passive (*passividade*), defined as feminine.

This ideology shapes the meanings of sexual relations between males and females and also between individuals of the same sex. The act of penetration of the female body by the male in sexual intercourse is the powerful act—in a concrete and metaphorical sense—that proclaims male superiority, linking male and female bodies in a relation of (male) dominance and (female) submission. Penetration symbolically expresses the hierarchical power relations at the heart of the patriarchal gender system. It is the central symbol of sexual relations and indeed, symbolically, all gender differences. Whether penetration actually occurs or is merely implied, it is key to the sex/gender system of Brazil.

The emphasis of the Brazilian sex/gender system is reflected—and reinforced—by the language with which Brazilians speak about the body and its practices and about sexuality and gender (Parker 1995:243). In common usage, position in sexual intercourse is expressed by the verbs "to eat" (*comer*) and "to give" (*dar*). Comer describes the male's active penetration and domination of the female and is used in different contexts as a synonym for the verbs "to possess" (*possuir*) or "to conquer" (*vencer*).

Dar is used to describe the female's passive submission to her male partner in her role of being penetrated during intercourse. Just as comer is used to describe various forms of domination through reference to the relations of gender, dar is also used to imply submission, subjugation, and passivity in varied contexts, from politics to sports, in which victors are said to have "eaten" their opponents. Thus, even the simplest verbal exchanges in Brazil reinforce the association of sexual atividade and passividade with relations of power and domination between men and women.

Through the act of eating, the active partner metaphorically consumes the passive, while through the act of giving, the passive partner offers herself/himself up to be possessed. The act of penetration thus also defines categories of persons: Husbands are associated with those who "eat," wives with those who "give."

GENDER DIVERSITY: TRAVESTÍS, BICHAS, AND VIADOS

This model of the relationship between males and females is central to Brazilian understandings of gender diversity, which focus on the effeminate passive male homosexual, who, depending on the region of Brazil and the social situation, is variously called *bicha* (literally bug, pest, or female animal), *viado* (literally, deer), or *travestí* (from the verb to cross-dress). Although these gender variants readily self-identify as homosexual, in the traditional sex/gender system, the term "homosexual" was not applied to the male-acting and penetrating partner in a same-sex sexual relationship. Thus, bichas, viados, and travesitís are "produced" through the application of the distinction between atividad and passividade to sexual relations between individuals of the same sex, not solely by virtue of their sexual orientation.

Because the most important criterion of the Brazilian sex/gender ideology is the sexual and social roles people play, not their sexual orientation, or even their biological sex (Fry 1986; Parker 1991), a male who enters into a sexual relationship with another male does not necessarily sacrifice his masculinity, so long as he performs the penetrating, active, masculine role during sexual intercourse and conducts himself as a male within society. The active male in same-sex sexual relations is an unmarked male—he falls into no special category of gender nonconformity. He does not regard himself as a homosexual and is not regarded as one by society. Same-sex sexual practices are reported as a common introduction to sexual activity for many Brazilian men during adolescence, and those in the active role are not stigmatized. Indeed, as part of the drive to dominate sexually, penetrating another male is sometimes claimed as an indication of a supervirile masculine identity (Parker 1995:245).

A male is a man (*homem* or *macho*) until he is accused of or proved to have "given" (i.e., taken the female role in sex), in which case he

Brazilian travestís are prominent in the festival of Carnival, which, like the American Mardi Gras, is particularly associated with inversion. (Photograph © Maria Weidner/ Shutterstock.com.)

becomes a bicha (or viado). If a male accepts that social role, he becomes a "real bicha." Taking on this role publicly is called *solta plumas*, literally "releases feathers" (from the importance of feathers in Carnival, the annual pre-Lenten period of revelry, similar to the American Mardi Gras), which is particularly associated with bichas because of the Carnival theme of inversion. A real bicha is assumed to be sexually a **passivo** (the man who takes the subordinate role in sexual relations in Brazil).

In Brazil, as in other "gender organized" systems of same-sex sexual relationships, the sexually receptive partner is expected to enact other aspects of the feminine gender role: to behave and/or sound and/or dress in ways appropriate to women. Once this role is imputed to an individual, it seriously damages his *masculinidade*, unalterably transforming and degrading him, as he becomes a symbolic female through his sexual role.

But bichas, viados, and travestís do not merely dress and act like women; they also transform their bodies (Kulick 1997, 1998). Boys who self-identify as travestís may begin ingesting or injecting female hormones as early as age 10 or 12, in order to develop breasts and give their bodies feminine contours. These hormones, which are either medications for combating estrogen deficiency in women or oral contraceptives, are cheap and available in Brazil. Travestís also use (most frequently industrial plastic) silicone for implants in order to create the fleshy thighs, expansive hips, and prominent buttocks that are the focus of the Brazilian ideal of feminine beauty (for a variety of aesthetic, practical, and medical reasons, silicone is not used for breast implants [Kulick 1997:576]).

In spite of their bodily modifications, however, travestís believe that a travestí is not a woman and can never be one, because "God created them male and their sex can never be changed" (Kulick 1998:193ff). This is a significant contrast to Western transsexuals, though similar in some ways to hijras, who also do not believe they can become women. Unlike hijras, travestís do not want to get rid of their penises; they believe that sex-change operations do not produce women, but only castrated homosexuals. Furthermore, travestís believe that without a penis semen cannot leave the body and the trapped semen will eventually travel to the brain and cause madness. Thus, in a seeming paradox, simultaneously with their determined desire for a feminine body, travestís value their male genitals and "gasp in horror" at the thought of an amputation, which would mean the loss of an ability to have an erection or an orgasm (Kulick 1997:577). In yet another seeming paradox, travestís keep their penises hidden, that is, "imprisoned" between their legs, also noted as a self-defining skill of hijras. This is an important travestí bodily practice in their daily public appearances, in their work as prostitutes, and in deference to their boyfriends' (*maridos*) masculine identities.

Unlike Western transsexuals, travestís modify their bodies not because they feel themselves to be women, but because they feel themselves to be "like women"—in their behavior, appearance, and particularly in their relationships with men (Kulick 1997:577). A common—and crucial—theme in travestís' identities is that they experience themselves as travestís in connection with their sexual attraction to men, specifically in their desire for, and participation in, anal penetration. This attraction motivates their feminized bodily modifications and is central to their occupation as prostitutes and to their intimate relations with their maridos. Unlike characterizations that abound in modern Euro-American culture, travestí relations with men are not characterized as homosexual; rather they are viewed as "heterogenderal," because the relationship is culturally defined by the social/sexual differences in gender, not by the sameness of (male) bodies and sexual orientation.

Travestís' maridos (like some hijras' husbands) are typically attractive, muscular, tattooed young men with little education or income. They are not pimps, although they are supported by the travestí; rather, they move in with the travestí for "passion" and are kicked out on the same basis. Maridos regard themselves, and are regarded by their travestí girlfriends, as men. Since one of the defining characteristics of a "man" is that he will not be interested in another male's penis, the marido keeps his manhood by penetrating the travestí. Although some travestís express pleasure in taking the active sexual role, they also claim that this role would then cause them to lose respect for the marido, who would be transformed into a viado, *bicha incubada* (incubating bicha) in their eyes (Kulick 1998:96ff; Fry 1995:205). When a bicha or travestí learns that her man "gives" and has thus become a bicha, the humiliation is intense; no self-respecting bicha would admit to being penetrated by another bicha. The occasional "anything goes" sexual relationship in which no clear line is drawn between the male who "eats" and the male who "gives" is looked down upon. It is jokingly—and derogatorily—called lesbianism, referring to the bichas' view that lesbians don't really have (proper) sex (Fry 1995:204). Thus, within the bicha/travestí subculture, the norms of the heterosexual world are replicated; masculinity is associated with penetration, and those who do not adhere to the active/passive distinction are stigmatized.

The verbalized commitment to this heterogender sexual norm sometimes contrasts, however, with actual behavior. On the streets travestís know they are valued for their possession of a penis; clients will often request to see or feel it before payment, and clients frequently request anal penetration. But even as travestís comply, they consider it an inversion of their normal practice and charge a higher price (Cornwall 1994:120).

MEN AND NOT-MEN: THE BRAZILIAN BINARY

Sex/gender diversity becomes meaningful only within each culture's distinctive sex/gender system. Thus, while travestís are not-men (or "failed men"), they are not, like hijras, considered an in-between or third gender, though they are sometimes described this way in the popular media. Nor are travestís considered as a kind of woman, either by themselves or by others, although as prostitutes they are symbolically and socially "fallen" women and as such are doubly victimized.

Anthropologist Don Kulick (1997:579) explains travestís in terms of a Brazilian sex/gender system based on a dichotomy whose opposing categories are not men and women but rather men and not-men. The travestís are the example *par excellence* that the Brazilian sex/gender dichotomy is based on sexuality, rather than anatomy.

While biological differences are hardly ignored in Brazil, the definition of gender depends not merely on the possession of genitals but on what they are used for. Travestís reiterate the Brazilian view that the locus of gender difference is the act of penetration. If one *only* penetrates, one is a man, but if one gets penetrated *one is not a man*; one is either a woman or a bicha/viado (Kulick 1997:580). The enjoyment of being penetrated classifies travestís with women: because they already share a gender with women (although they make no claims to be women), they do not need to change their sex. Losing their penises would add nothing and would be a loss of both pleasure and income.

Since travestís are classified with (not as) women, they are expected to share all the qualities of women, particularly the desire to attract and be attractive to persons of the opposite gender (men). An important part of this attraction—for women as for travestís—is as a subject for the male gaze: In Brazil, female bodies are extraordinarily looked at, and men do the looking. This emphasis on the importance of a bodily aesthetic in sexual relations and definitions of gender leads travestís to make extravagant attempts to incorporate Brazilian cultural ideals of beauty in their bodies, drawing them not to resistance but to reinforcement of the dominant patriarchal and hierarchical sex/gender system of which they are a part.

ATTITUDES TOWARD GENDER DIVERSITY

Attitudes toward gender diversity in Brazil are best described as complex, sometimes contradictory, and ambivalent. Gender diversity is central to Carnival, itself a positive icon of Brazilian culture both to

Brazilians themselves and to the outside world. In Carnival, cross-dressing and gender inversion are prominent, not only for travestís, but also for gender-conforming men. Travestís often appear in Brazilian television soap operas, and Brazilians' open attitudes toward sexuality are reflected in the apparently universal willingness of men in Brazil to publicly admire the travestí, Roberta Close (who subsequently became a transsexual), as the most beautiful woman in Brazil (Kottak 1990).

At the same time that some travestís may be cultural icons, however, most travestís are actually treated very badly. In upsetting the culturally prescribed fit between biological sex and social gender, bichas, viados, and travestís are perceived as failed men, not as women. Thus, they are viewed and severely stigmatized as a failure on both social and biological counts: Unable to realize their biological potential as men because of inappropriate sexual behavior, they are equally unable to cross the boundaries of gender due to their inability to reproduce.

Travestís and bichas tend to be ostracized in mainstream society and find employment only in highly marginal lines of work or in jobs traditionally reserved for women. In some parts of Brazil they are called *marginais*, a term whose meaning of "marginal" is much stronger than its English translation. They are associated not only with sexually deviant behavior but with criminality and have been noted by several anthropologists as being among the most marginalized, feared, and despised groups in Brazil (Cornwall 1994; Kulick 1996:4; 1998). Travestís are regularly victims of police brutality and even murder, and until recently, many would not come out of doors during the day and were confined to the worst areas of cities. Most come from very poor backgrounds, and many have severe health and drug abuse problems. Travestís do engage in criminal acts, mainly their well-known practice of robbing their customers, and their association with homosexuality, prostitution, and now AIDS increases the stigma and censure they experience. In the streets often they are addressed mockingly as "Mister," a contemptuous way of refusing to acknowledge their gender.

The harshest scorn is reserved for unattractive travestís. Anthropologist Don Kulick (1998) suggests that perhaps the harassment on the street, which takes the form of verbally mocking travestís' gender as "not-men," is less a reaction to them as gender-crossers than a reaction against unattractiveness in people (women and other not-men) whose job it is to make themselves attractive to men. Travestís like Roberta Close and others who meet or even exceed Brazilian ideals of feminine beauty are not mocked, and ordinary men even seem willing to acknowledge them as legitimate sexual objects (Kottak 1990). Thus, in yet another permutation in the Brazilian sex/gender system, some of the hostility against travestís may be a reaction against them as failed women, not failed men.

AFRO-BRAZILIAN RELIGION

Gender diversity in Brazil is associated with Afro-Brazilian religions. While passivos are generally stigmatized in Latin America, women and passivos dominate the leadership in Afro-Brazilian religions. These religions, focused on possession trance (a state in which a spirit enters the human body) and oriented toward providing spiritual help and protection for their followers, are found predominantly in the north and northeast regions of Brazil, areas that contain a majority of African-Brazilians and the poor, and where gender relationships are generally more rigid than in the industrialized, more highly educated, and more socially mobile urbanized south.

The most familiar Afro-Brazilian religions are called **Candomble** (or Macumba) (see Fry 1995; Wafer 1991). Their main spirits are *orixas* of West African, primarily Yoruba, origin, who are also identified with saints of the Roman Catholic Church. This syncretism developed dur-

Women and male gender variants occupy important roles in Yoruba possession religions, which spread to the New World. (Photograph by Serena Nanda.)

ing the colonial period in Brazil, when the slaves concealed their African gods behind the masks of Christian saints. Under the leadership of the major orixas are a host of lesser spirits essential to day-to-day ritual activity. Candomble is organized into houses called *terreiros,* which are hierarchically structured around a female or male leader called mother or father of the saint. Each terreiro is autonomous and competes against other terreiros for followers, clients, and resources.

Candomble practitioners or followers are called sons- or daughters-of-saints and owe their allegiance to the particular mother- or father-of-saint of their chosen terreiro. Thus, the terreiro operates as a hierarchically organized extended family with allegiance and obligation being the duty of the followers and guidance and spiritual care the responsibility of the leader. Within the terreiro women as well as men may assume the role of patriarchal family head, and the father- or mother-of-saints maintains control over the followers. The modeling of the terreiro on the kinship structure of a family proscribes sexual relations among the followers and between the followers and the terreiro leaders.

Candomble religious life is expressed in public dances and festivals, ritual offerings, divinatory sessions, and initiation rituals, all of which involve the participation of diverse spirits. Various rituals and services are also provided for nonpracticing believers, who approach the religion as clients in search of spiritual assistance. The most significant ritual event is initiation, which centers around possession trance. Once initiated, a follower is obligated to his or her possessing spirits and patron deities who are called on to guarantee good fortune, health, success, and survival. The member's obligation to the orixas requires regular offerings, but most important, the follower must "receive" (*receber*) the orixas in regular ritual séances, which take the form of possession trances (Hayes 1996:15).

Possession trance or "receiving the spirits" establishes contact between the human realm and the divine and transforms initiates into followers of the saints, distinguishing them from clients and spectators. Other, noninitiated terreiro members act as ritual assistants or drummers, or perform the animal sacrifices that are a source of the sacrificial blood necessary to nourish the gods. Spirits ritually inhabit the body of a follower in possession trance, as well as inhabiting his or her special "altar," a collection of symbolic representations of the spirit that contain the spirit's power. The medium dances while possessed and also speaks with clients, giving advice and ritual protection. Theatricality is an important aspect of the performance, and terreiros are elaborately decorated with statues of spirits, paper flags and streamers, flashing lights, and so forth. Mediums are expected to dress well, and terreiro members pride themselves in their singing and dancing skills. The ritual ends with the departure of the spirits, although mediums may remain possessed for hours or even days afterward (Hayes 1996).

LINKS BETWEEN CANDOMBLE
AND GENDER DIVERSITY

Early descriptions of Afro-Brazilian religions noted the predominance of women as religious leaders, emphasizing the warm and nurturing qualities of women as central to the spiritual services that the cults offered (Landes 1946). After the 1940s, however, Candomble leaders were increasingly effeminate passivos. Although some observers criticized this shift as a corruption of traditional Yoruba "matriarchy," Candomble's association with gender diversity appears to be consistent with the sexual ambiguity that characterizes Yoruba religion in its homeland (Matory 1996). Among the Yoruba, transvestism, feminine gestures, and feminine occupations are marked among male possession priests (Matory 1994:170ff). During and soon after initiation, Yoruba possession priests are called brides of the god and don women's clothing during initiation. Both male and female priests wear feminine hairstyles and feminine cosmetics and jewelry.

The view that the passivo presence in Candomble continues rather than disrupts Yoruba tradition complements earlier functionalist explanations of the association between passivos and Afro-Brazilian possession religions. Several of these explanations focus on marginality. Although even upper-class Brazilians seek the magical services of Candomble, Afro-Brazilian religions are considered deviant in the dominant Brazilian culture (in the past, these religions were outlawed by the Brazilian government; this has changed as the government now views the Afro-Brazilian religions as an important tourist attraction). The negative association of Candomble with the poor and with the "superstitiousness" of African religions, as well as with haunts of immorality and crime, make Candomble practitioners socially and spatially marginal in Brazilian society. Terreiros, for example, are most often located on the outskirts of cities and are difficult to find.

Thus, one widespread explanation for the association of Candomble with passivos, and indeed, more widely with "deviant" sexuality as well as with women, suggests the cults provide a cultural space where women and passivos, stigmatized and oppressed in the larger society, can exercise spiritual powers from which they receive otherwise unavailable financial and social rewards (Fry 1986). Another functional explanation for the association of gender nonconformists with Afro-Brazilian religions is that in the terreiro and its activities, passivos may give rein to their "femininity" through association with the predominantly female membership of the religions and through possession by female spirits (Fry 1986). Additionally, once the religious leadership becomes associated in the popular imagination with passivos for whatever reasons, other men will not want to risk their masculinity by being associated with Afro-Brazilian religious leadership (Fry 1995:201).

Anthropologist Peter Fry also suggests that since both passivos and possession trance religions are defined as deviant in relation to dominant Brazilian values, marginal individuals can find a congenial role in them. More particularly, he notes, the very deviance of the passivos enhances their ability to be religious leaders: To be defined by society as defiling and dangerous may be an advantage to those in a role in which they exercise magical power. In this sense, Fry views passivos as having an advantage over both women and men as Candomble leaders (Fry 1995:195). The enhanced magical power of passivos comes from being associated with the potential destructiveness, yet also with the power of "disorder," that occurs in the meeting of the secular and the divine. Like hijras and Native American gender variants, the relation of magical power to the margins of society is easily associated with those defined as sexually ambiguous.

Other explanations of passivo success in Candomble emphasize that it is the *combination* of the masculine and the feminine that gives them an advantage (Fry 1995:207). J. Lorand Matory notes that in Afro-Brazilian religions, despite the important presence of women priest-esses, the gender of the divine agency defining the priestess's authority is often male. Passivos enjoy some of the unique ritual prerogatives of men in Candomble and also are not subject to the prohibitions placed on the participation of menstruating women (Matory 1996:23). While both men and women must cleanse themselves from the pollution of sexual relations before and during ritual activity, passivos are subject only to the lesser defilement of males and are more easily cleansed than women.

Yet, at the same time, passivos, as women, are exempt from the taboos on males engaging in cooking and embroidery, both of which are important to the success of the terreiro. In addition, passivos do not have the obligations of marriage and kinship and can thus devote all their earn-ings to the terreiro, increasing its material display and thus enhancing confidence in its efficacy and winning larger numbers of committed follow-ers. Passivos are also considered more artistic than either men or women and are therefore perceived as better equipped to organize and participate in ritual activity. Passivos thus are not merely a "pale imitation of a woman," but rather combine certain key aspects of the "normal" male and female roles, which they can manipulate to their own advantage.

PENETRATION, POSSESSION TRANCE, AND GENDER DIVERSITY IN CANDOMBLE

Symbolic explanations for passivo predominance in Candomble are also relevant. The meanings of penetration and possession in Candomble both reinforce and resist the dominant norms of gendered relationships in Brazil and help explain the association of Candomble with women and passivos (Hayes 1996). In Candomble the relationship between the spirits and humans—between the gods and the followers who incorporate them—is analogically associated with that of male-to-females through the metaphor of penetration. Thus, the term describing possession is *dar santo* (to give saint): The role of the human being (whether man or woman) possessed by the spirit in trance—"possession trance"—is identified with the female who gives herself over to sexual penetration by the male. The Candomble priests who are possessed are called "horses" or "mounts" of the gods, who "ride" them, again recalling the submissive or passive role of women in sexual relations. During possession, the god "mounts" the priest, as a rider does a horse or as a male does his female sexual partner. The role of metaphorical male in this relation between humans and spirits is occupied by the spirits, who *penetrate*, who ride their mounts (*cavalos*: horses) in order to express their desires, chastise their followers, advise, or merely to "play." This makes sense of the fact that women—and passivos—are more appropriate for the role of *filho-de-santos* (followers-of-the-saints) than men.

If women, who receive the gods in trance, thus mimic the normative male–female relations in which penetration (spiritual or sexual) defines them as female, it follows that men who are ridden by the gods are deemed passivo, for they assume the female role of being penetrated as opposed to the normative male role of penetration. Thus, spiritual penetration by the (male) gods for a male is equivalent to becoming a passivo: It involves a renunciation of masculine (atividade) in favor of the most passive role, that of *dando santo* (giving saint). As anthropologist Jim Wafer describes it (1991:18), humans are "female" in relation to all the spirits when they go into possession trance. Humans "give" offerings so that the spirits may "eat."

In the religious context of possession trance, then, normative gender relationships are reiterated and reinforced. Even as possession trance reiterates normative gender classifications, it furthermore reinterprets and reevaluates them (Hayes 1996). Within the religious context, being penetrated is empowering rather than subordinating, and it is prestigious rather than degraded (if only because of the high status of the gods in relation to humans). This helps explain the attraction of women and passivos to the Afro-Brazilian possession religions. In this respect, possession trance is similar to other religious situations that have long been associated with alternative interpretations and revaluations of social reality. This association creates situations in which normative systems of classification may be questioned, violated, manipulated, or reversed and in which those who are marginal in the real world become central in religious ritual (see Turner 1969).

CHANGING SEX/GENDER IDEOLOGIES

In Brazil, as increasingly in many contemporary cultures, several sex/gender ideologies coexist. Along with the traditional emphasis on sexual practice as determinative of gender identity, a modern Euro-American "medical" model of sex/gender relations entered Brazil in the late-nineteenth and early-twentieth centuries that emphasized same-sex sexual relations as detrimental to the health of society (Parker 1999). This model still exists, but in the last three decades it has been challenged by a (postmodern) gay ideology, in which both partners in a same-sex sexual relationship are viewed equally in terms of their sexual orientation. This current model continues the homosexual/heterosexual divide of the medical model, but without its pejorative connotations. It has particularly gained a foothold in the more highly industrialized urban centers of southern Brazil (Rio and Sao Paulo) as well as among the more wealthy and educated classes throughout Brazil. The traditional pattern continues to dominate in the north and northeast among the rural, less-educated, and poorer classes. Brazil, then, like Thailand and the Philippines, is most accurately characterized as having not one but several sex/gender ideologies, related to each other in complex and sometimes contradictory ways.

Review and Reflection

1. Explain the traditional basis of Brazilian gender ideology and describe how it affects Brazil's system of sex/gender diversity.

2. Discuss the relationship between Candomble, the Yoruba religion, and the gender diverse role of the passivo.

3. Explain how you would evaluate Brazil's social response to gender diversity as positive, negative, or ambivalent, using specific examples from the chapter.

4. Analyze the roles of travestís in Brazilian society and explain some of the contradictory ways they define themselves.

5. How is "homosexuality" defined in Brazilian culture? (Looking ahead: Compare this with the contemporary definition of homosexuality in United States culture.)

6. Judge the importance of specific sexual acts, for example, penetration, in defining gender in Brazil. (Looking back: How does this compare with its importance in defining the hijras in Bangladesh?)

7. Looking ahead: Compare and contrast the Brazilian travestí to the Indonesian waria. How are they similar and how are they different?

Chapter Four

Liminal Gender Roles
in Polynesia

Polynesia, the "many islands" of the Pacific, are commonly differentiated from the Pacific islands of Melanesia. While individuals of "in-between" sex/gender are acknowledged and linguistically marked in Melanesia (see Herdt 1996b), and while a central part of male initiation involves young boys ingesting semen from older males in order to become masculine, this ritual is not associated with sex/gender diversity (Herdt 1981). In contrast, there are long-standing, deep-rooted, and many various traditions of sex/gender diversity in Polynesia (Besnier and Alexeyeff in press).

The local economies of Polynesia primarily depend on horticulture and products of the sea, though a cash economy is now also important almost everywhere. The more complex Polynesian societies are characterized by social ranking systems consisting of chiefs, nobles, and commoners. Rank is determined by position—birth order and genealogical closeness to the chief—and kinship is thus an essential source of political, economic, and social power. Competition for power and prestige is a central cultural preoccupation for men, although women, too, have informal avenues of influence. Traditionally, elaborate systems of taboos restricted interaction between different social categories, including men and women, and these rules influence behavior even today.

Gender relations in Polynesia are complementary, with men and women having their own spheres of work, sociality, and behavioral norms, though the intensity of gender role differentiation varies among the islands. Two important widespread gender norms in Polynesia are respect relationships between brothers and sisters (or those classified as such, i.e., males and females of the same generation) and the division of women's roles into the more positively valued virginal "girl," and the less valued, mature wife, who has had at least one child (Mageo 1992; Shore 1981).

Polynesia has, since its discovery by Europeans, figured in the Western imagination as a place of unrestricted and casual sexuality, including a "tolerance" of gender diversity. Yet, expressions of sexuality in Polynesia are, as in all societies, culturally shaped and constrained. Sexual expression, gender relations, and attitudes toward gender diversity are all grounded in the Polynesian cultural emphasis on the contrast between socially controlled and uncontrolled aspects of human existence. "Good" behavior is that which conforms to social roles and is characterized by respect and restraint of personal impulses. "Bad," "disgusting," and "selfish" behavior is that which is motivated by personal desire, impulsiveness, and self-gratification (Shore 1981:195). Sexuality, in particular, is associated with personal desire.

The values of social role and emotional and behavioral restraint are exemplified in many aspects of Polynesian sexuality and gender relations: the idealization of virginity; a distinction between women as wives and women as sisters; and the importance of kinship relations, particularly those between brother and sister, as the basis for appropriate, and restrained, social and sexual interaction. Gender diversity in Polynesia needs to be understood within the context of these (and other) cultural patterns, discussed below.

GENDER LIMINAL MALE ROLES

The main cultural feature of gender diversity in Polynesia, though this differs among islands, involves males who take on certain feminine characteristics, a pattern both traditional and deeply embedded in much of Polynesia. These gender variant roles have different names in different places, reflecting Polynesian cultural variation (Besnier 1996). In Tahiti and contemporary Hawai'i, the role is called *māhū*. (Although there is little historical documentation of female māhū in Tahiti, these roles may also be occupied by women [Elliston 1999]). In Samoa, male gender variants are called *fa'afafine*, which literally means "like a woman"; in Tonga, the term is *fakaleitī*, whose root, *leitī*, is borrowed from the English word "lady"; and in Tuva in the Gilbertese islands, the term is *pinapinaaine*.

In spite of the long history and wide distribution of sex/gender diversity in Polynesia there is no consistently articulated ideology associated with sex/gender variants; they are not identified with a uniformly consistent role; and the boundaries of the role are "porous": A man can move into the role and then move out of it in later life. In Poly-

Hermaphrodite fig-
ures, combining male
and female anatomy,
play an important role
in creation stories all
over the Pacific islands.
(Photograph by
Ravinder Nanda.)

nesian social life, behavior and identity are generally a matter of appropriate situational context, and this is also true for the enactment of
gender diversity. This accounts for the substantial variability among
gender variant individuals and also variability in an individual's
behavior in different situations and over a lifetime (Besnier 1996). At
the same time, in some places, for example Tahiti, social acceptance of
a gender variant individual is significantly legitimated by his long-
term participation in this role, frequently manifested since childhood
(Elliston 1999:236).

Because of cultural and individual variation, defining Polynesian
gender diversity is problematic. Although *māhū* is translated in Tahiti
as "half-man, half-woman," māhū are not considered to be a well-
defined third gender like hijras are in India or like the gender variants
are among Native Americans. Deborah Elliston (1999:236) defines
māhū in Tahiti "as a gender category for persons who deploy and participate in complex combinations of masculine and feminine gender
signs and practices," with the dominant gender role being that which is
opposite to the individual's anatomy.

Regarding male gender diversity in Polynesia generally, the most important of these "gender signs and practices" appears to be engaging in women's work. Other important feminine gender markers adopted by males are feminine dress, speech tones and nonverbal gestures, and dance styles. Also noteworthy is the association of gender-nonconforming males with girls and young women in friendship groups, which, given the importance of sex-segregated social gatherings in Polynesia, is significant.

Although sexuality (sexual orientation or sexual practices) does not define Polynesian gender diversity, gender variant sexuality is assumed to be consistent with the adopted gender, with males taking male sexual partners and females taking female lovers. Gender variant males in Tonga, for example, are stereotypically associated with certain sexual practices, acting as "receivers" in oral and anal sex and defining straight men as objects of their erotic desires (Besnier 2011:143). Gay and leitī are strongly differentiated however; indeed, until recently the concept "gay," which is associated with the West, was almost unknown in Tonga; even today it is not completely understood.

In contrast to India, Native North America, and Indonesia, Polynesian gender diversity is not generally associated with sacred powers, although māhū in Hawai'i were traditionally recognized as experts in hula, Hawaiian crafts, lei making, chanting and singing—all of which were important cultural features of Hawaiian life (Matzner 2001). With the domination of Hawai'i by Christian missionaries in the nineteenth and twentieth centuries, however, the māhū role, like so much else of Hawaiian culture, came under threat and almost disappeared in its traditional form. Today, māhū may still be teased and harassed and the term still has some negative connotations, but both the role and the individuals to which the term "māhū" refers are also enjoying something of a renaissance as part of the contemporary revitalization of traditional Hawaiian culture (Xian 2001).

In Polynesia generally, though sex/gender diversity is not associated with particular expertise in traditional cultural skills, as in Hawai'i, it is associated with "rituals of reversal," secular cultural performances that involve spontaneous clowning and uninhibited behavior that is normally disparaged and repressed. These performances are an important way that gender diversity is functionally integrated into some Polynesian societies. Given the high variability in gender variant roles, the marginality of gender variant persons in Polynesian societies, their association with "rituals of reversal," and the limited contexts in which gender diversity is enacted, ethnographer Niko Besnier suggests that the term "gender liminal" or "transgender" are the most accurate ways to define their cultural status. The term "liminal"—in-between—especially suggests that Polynesian gender variants mainly derive their meaning in society from the normative Polynesian binary gender system of man and woman, rather than from any distinctive features or an independent status of their own.

As in Brazil, the Polynesian gender liminal individual crosses genders in acting "like a woman" but is not viewed as having become a woman. He is rather suspended between man and woman, being neither, and at the same time having elements of both. Since kinship in Polynesia is structured on the basis of a fundamental opposition and hierarchical complementarity between male and female roles, there is no room for an autonomous, institutionalized in-between gender. Thus, gender liminal individuals are men who *borrow* certain social and cultural attributes and symbols normatively associated with women. These attributes may differ in kind and number and may be foregrounded or backgrounded in different contexts, even occasionally shed if needed. This borrowing is the process that gives rise to a loosely defined gender liminal identity that is treated rather casually by the society. And because of the importance of kinship in Polynesia, gender liminal individuals remain embedded in this system and so, while marginalized, are not rejected and left on their own as are Indian hijras or to some extent Indonesian waria.

HISTORICAL CONTEXTS

The earliest Europeans to reach Polynesia in the late-eighteenth century noted and commented on gender diversity, although missionaries in the nineteenth and early-twentieth centuries by and large did not. European colonial regimes differed in Polynesia but in most cases attempted to suppress what gender diversity they found, although today, some mainstream Tongans claim that leitī sexuality in fact resulted from "Western" influence (Besnier 2010: 145), a common enough claim for culture traits that locals are ambivalent about. Anthropologists in the early-twentieth century hardly mentioned the subject. As with other aspects of Polynesian sexuality, the social "acceptance" of gender diversity tended to be romanticized in some anthropological accounts in the mid-1950s, as well as in later accounts by Western gay observers. Only in the 1970s did some relatively detailed ethnography on Polynesian gender diversity begin to make its appearance. Thus, it is not clear whether contemporary gender liminality in Polynesia represents continuity with gender liminality in the past or a break from the past and a new cultural construction.

As in Native North America, the Europeans who first encountered Polynesia immediately noticed the presence of gender diversity and associated it with their own concept of homosexual sodomy, as in this eighteenth-century account (below) from Tahiti (note the comparison the writer makes with the eunuchs—possibly he means hijras here—of India, who were already well-known and much commented on by European travelers):

> "[The māhū] are like the Eunichs [sic] in India but they are not castrated. They never cohabit with women but live as they do. They pick their beards out and dress as women, dance and sing with them and are as effeminate in their voice. They do women's employment and excell [sic] in some crafts. It is said that they converse with men as familiar as women do." (Morrison, quoted in Levy 1973:130)

Captain Bligh, commander of the *Bounty*, infamous because of the mutiny of its crew, also noted the behavior of the māhū, observing that they participated in the same ceremonies as women and ate as women did. The māhū's effeminate speech led Bligh to believe they were castrated, but he later found out that they were not, noting, however, that "things equally disgusting were committed" (referring to their sexual relations with men). Bligh was told that the māhū were selected when they were boys and kept with the women solely for "the caresses of the men." When, in order to learn more about them, Bligh had one māhū remove his loincloth, he noted:

> "He had the appearance of a woman, his yard [penis] and testicles being so drawn in under him, having the art from custom of keeping them in this position . . . [His genitals] are very small and the testicles remarkably so, being not larger than a boy's five or six years old, and very soft as in a state of decay or a total incapacity of being larger, so that . . . he appeared . . . a Eunuch [as much as if] his stones were away. The women treat him as one of their sex and he observed every restriction that they do, and is equally respected and esteemed." (Bligh, quoted in Levy 1973:130–31)

Bligh goes on to report that the men who had sexual relations with a māhū "have their beastly pleasures gratified between his thighs" but they denied practicing sodomy. A nineteenth-century account declared that a māhū fellated the man he had relations with, swallowing the semen, which was believed to give them strength (Levy 1973:135). Contemporary accounts note similar behavior, and some Tahitian men talk of the exceptional strength of māhū.

APPROPRIATIONS OF THE FEMININE

The defining criterion for a māhū is that he *publicly* engages in the occupations and activities of women. In one Tahitian rural district, ethnographer Robert Levy noted that the māhū's "feminine role taking is demonstrated for the villagers because he performs women's household activities, cleans the house, takes care of babies, braids coconut palm leaves into thatching plaits" (1973:140). A māhū in another district associates with the adolescent girls of the village and walks with his arm interlocked with theirs, "a behavior otherwise seen only among people of the same sex."

In Polynesia women and men play different economic roles. In Samoa, for example, males do the "heavy" and instrumental work of directly providing food, whether from gardening or from the sea, while women are linked with "light" work that is largely decorative and associated with the household and the village, such as keeping the village clean and weaving the fine mats that are used in Polynesian rituals of exchange (Mead 1971; Shore 1981:203). Gender-nonconforming males do the light work of women and, as among Native Americans, are thought to excel in women's occupations. In urban areas of Polynesia, gender nonconformists are considered excellent secretaries and are coveted domestic help (Besnier 1997).

Polynesian gender distinctions of dress may seem small to Westerners but are important gender markers. In Samoa, for example, gendered dress styles are well defined, particularly in the way the *lavalava* (sarong) is tied (Shore 1981:206). Although men and women may use the same material and colors, men leave a large end of their lavalava flopping in the front. Women, in contrast, do not let the end hang out, but rather tuck the end inside the waist. Thus, a man can convey a gender transformation by consistently tying his lavalava in a feminine style. Although gender variants are often referred to as "transvestites" in the anthropological accounts of Polynesia, they generally do not cross-dress on a permanent basis; however cross-dressing does provide a vehicle of self-identification and social presentation for gender variant males (and females). In Tahiti, Elliston reports (1999:236) that most male māhū consistently wear *pareus* (garments worn mainly by women), but in other parts of Polynesia much of the gender variant males' transvestism occurs within the context of stage performances.

Speech differences associated with men and women in Polynesian societies are also a vehicle for gender variation. Male gender variants adopt women's speech patterns and their "high pitched" tone of voice. Like women, transgender males act "coquettishly," are excessively concerned with their physical appearance, and often wear flowers, garlands, perfume, and heavy makeup like women. Other "feminine" characteristics include a feminine manner of walking and feminine gestures.

The performative emphasis in Polynesian culture underlines the view that gender variant statuses there are not necessarily permanent. For example, although Tahitians generally claim that changing one's sex is not possible, it is possible to stop being a māhū, "as one can discontinue being a chief." Anthropologist Robert Levy noted that in the village he studied, one man in his early adolescence had dressed from time to time in girls' clothes and was thus considered a māhū but in his early twenties "cast off" the role. It was assumed in the village that this was the end of it and that the person was now leading an ordinary masculine life (Levy 1973:133). At the same time, māhū are generally described as "natural" and thought to "have been born that way," in contrast to the nontraditional category of "homosexuals" who are believed to choose their roles when they are adults.

SEXUALITY AND GENDER LIMINALITY

Although it was the sexual behavior of the māhū in Tahiti that drew immediate and disapproving attention from Europeans, it is clear from both historical and contemporary accounts that the māhū role involved, and involves today, more than homoerotic desire and behavior (Besnier 1996; Elliston 1999; Shore 1981), which, in any case, by themselves do not define Polynesian transgenderism; as Deborah Elliston (1999:236) notes, a māhū is consistently associated with gender and his sexuality is consistently backgrounded. As in many cultures, men who have sexual relations with māhū are not considered to be gender variants themselves.

Nevertheless, Polynesian gender diversity *is* associated with a particular sexuality, however backgrounded. A māhū, fakaleitī, or pinapinaaine is the fellator and, as such, is seen as a substitute for a woman. While no stigma or shame is attached to a māhū's sexual partners, there is a potentially negative connotation that a person who seeks a māhū or his equivalent for a sexual partner does so because he cannot obtain a woman.

As earlier noted, transgender Polynesians are strongly differentiated from homosexuals. In contemporary Tahiti, homosexuality, called *raerae*, is considered a foreign (French) import and is differentiated from sexual relations with a māhū. Raerae refers to a person "who does not perform a female's village role and who dresses and acts like a man, but who indulges in exclusive or preferred sexual behavior with other men." Though there is some confusion over terms and categories, raerae seems to mean "sex-role reversal" and/or "sodomy"; it is also applied to a reversed role in sexual relations between a man and a woman (Levy 1973:140). While effeminate men may be described as māhūish, such an individual is assumed to be an ordinary man, involved in standard male activity, and engaged in normal heterosexual practices. In Samoa, there is no word for homosexual, and in any case, same-sex sexual play is viewed as part of a normal growing-up process for most boys (Mead 1971; Shore 1981).

The gender liminal role in Polynesia is not in any way imposed on men perceived as effeminate (in Polynesian terms), and it is unclear whether a physical anomaly is involved in recruitment to these roles. In Tahiti, one of Levy's māhū informants said that māhū are not supercised (a traditional coming-of-age ceremony for boys that involves incisions made on the shaft of the penis) because a māhū's penis is too small, an observation made in the early contact period. On the other hand, based on one observation, Levy expressed the view that diminutive genital size is not necessarily a physical correlate for the māhū role and that a boy might be "coached" into the role by his elders, perhaps just for their amusement, by dressing him in girls' clothes. If a male child seems determined to wear girls' clothes, adults will not stand in his way, and a child's insistence in some cases is felt to be "irresistible" (Levy 1973:140).

In Samoa, also, gender nonconformity might well begin in childhood, and a family with few girls may even bring up a boy child as a girl, though most gender variant boys adopt transvestism voluntarily (Mageo 1992:450). Contrary to the benign image presented by Levy for Tahiti, in Samoa a boy's male relatives may beat him for wearing girls' clothes, though potential fa'afafine may receive support from their mothers who, as supervisors of the household, are more likely than men to notice—and condone—the young boy's preference for women's domestic chores.

In traditional Polynesia, a preference for same-sex sexual intimacy was not considered either a necessary or sufficient criterion for gender liminal status. Intimate and erotic same-sex sexual behavior by itself does not "brand" one as a gender variant. In fact it is expected to, and frequently does, occur in other contexts such as boarding schools or prisons, and sexual experimentation among teenaged boys appears to be a normal part of Polynesian development. Gender liminal adult males are not presupposed to have a history of or an identifiable preference for same-sex sexual relationships; indeed, the "assignment" of gender liminal status frequently takes place in childhood, before the awakening of sexual desires. Rather, in common with Native North American gender variants, in Polynesia, sexual relations with men seem to be a possible *consequence* of a gender-nonconforming male status, rather than its cause, prerequisite, or primary attribute (Besnier 1996; Elliston 1999).

The association of specific kinds of sexual behavior with gender liminality in Polynesia is unclear. Levy noted that māhū perform fellatio on non-māhū, who view māhū to be a convenient, pleasurable, relatively pressure-free alternative to women for the release of sexual tension. In Tonga and Tuvalu, Besnier reports that young men brag in private about anally penetrating the gender divergent male and engaging in sex between his thighs; although Besnier notes māhū take the "female" role in sexual relations "as recipient rather than inserter" (1997:9), he reports elsewhere that transgender males do sometimes act as inserters. A Polynesian male (as in India and Brazil) who takes the inserter position with another male is not linguistically distinguished or socially marginalized. Because this practice is somewhat stigmatized as conveying an inability to find a woman, however, it is mainly associated with younger men. Married men are assumed to have sex only with women. And, similar to India, Brazil, Thailand, and the Philippines, gender nonconformists do not have sex with each other.

SEXUALITY AND SOCIAL STATUS

In spite of the "respect" that early Europeans attributed to gender liminal roles in traditional Polynesian societies, and in spite of their acceptance as "natural," today these roles do carry some social stigma, and the terms that define them can be, and often are, used derogatorily. This stigma, as well as the harassment and even the violence sometimes directed at gender variant individuals in some Polynesian societies, for example Tonga, is closely associated with their sexuality, which today, in contrast to the past, is becoming central to the definition of gender liminality (Besnier 1997).

Gender liminals are almost always perceived as possible subjects of sexual conquest by men in Polynesia, although paradoxically, in Tonga, for example, fakaleitī may also be viewed as sexual predators. In addition, while men must repay sexual favors from women with material goods, it is the fakaleitī who must spend money on his boyfriends for liquor, entertainment, and high-prestige consumer items (Besnier 1997:16). In Samoa and Tahiti fa'afafine or māhū may tease men in the same flirtatious way that women do, but even when not initiating a flirtation, they frequently will be the target of harassment and even physical violence, particularly from men in various states of inebriation (Besnier 1997). Gender liminal males are viewed as sexual "fair game" in a broader sense than women, who are to some extent protected by the classificatory brother–sister relationships so important in Polynesian kinship. This is particularly true for low-ranking gender liminal males; in Polynesian cultures, where social ranking is central to social structure, higher-ranking gender liminal males are somewhat protected by their social position.

The stigmatizing of the gender liminal male is related to his feminine role in sexual relations. While sexual position (inserter or insertee) is not reported as a critical marker of female inferiority in Polynesia, as it is in Brazil, outside of special circumstances, such as in prison, a gender-conforming male would not take an insertee role, because it would mean that he would be subordinating himself to another, which "no man in his right mind would consent to." Male gender liminality is also stigmatized in Polynesia because it is viewed as inherently promiscuous, transient, and lacking in significance. As Besnier so poignantly notes, "The gender liminal sexual partner, like the woman of loose virtue, is considered an eminently discardable and exploitable object" (1996:303). In Fiji, the gender liminal male as a sexual partner is analogized to a local, one-stringed musical instrument, whose tune is easily manipulated.

Besnier further notes that in Polynesia the sexuality of transgender males, unlike women, is socially defined as falling outside the erotic, expressed by a popular view that they "lack the sexual anatomy of a normal adult man," with genitals "too small for circumcision," though there is no real evidence of what seems an inaccurate stereotype. This stereotype may function however, to exclude gender liminals from adult erotic possibilities. They are, like children, held to be incapable of experiencing sexual desire, and the popular, though again inaccurate, view is that the "sole purpose of the encounter" for gender liminal males is to satisfy the sexual needs of their partners.

Gender liminal male sexuality in Polynesia, then, contains some contradictions: Gender liminals are significantly defined by their sexuality yet also traditionally known by their feminine occupations; they are considered both as falling outside the range of normal adult male eroticism and as being sexual predators; and they are like women in their sexual practices but are unlike women in that they pay for sexual favors. These contradictions are explained partly by Polynesian cultural variability, partly by the Polynesian concept of the person (discussed below), and partly by the public's ambivalence toward them.

PERFORMING GENDER DIVERSITY

Gender liminal roles in Polynesia are particularly closely associated with secular performances and entertainment, the forms and functions of which are rooted in the culture, social structure, and gender relations of these societies. This seems true for both traditional and contemporary performances, where transgender males are associated with spontaneous clowning and comic exaggerations. Perhaps because of the emphasis on role playing as a central and valued part of Polynesian life, gender variance also has aspects of a role that is being played and, indeed, is largely played on stage. A contemporary expression of these performances in Tonga, for example, is central to the transgender "Miss Galaxy" beauty contests, which attract wide audiences but lack the prestige of the Miss Heilala beauty pageants that emphasize local culture and are endorsed by the Tongan elite and official hierarchy. The Miss Galaxy contests on the other hand, are identified with a modern, global,

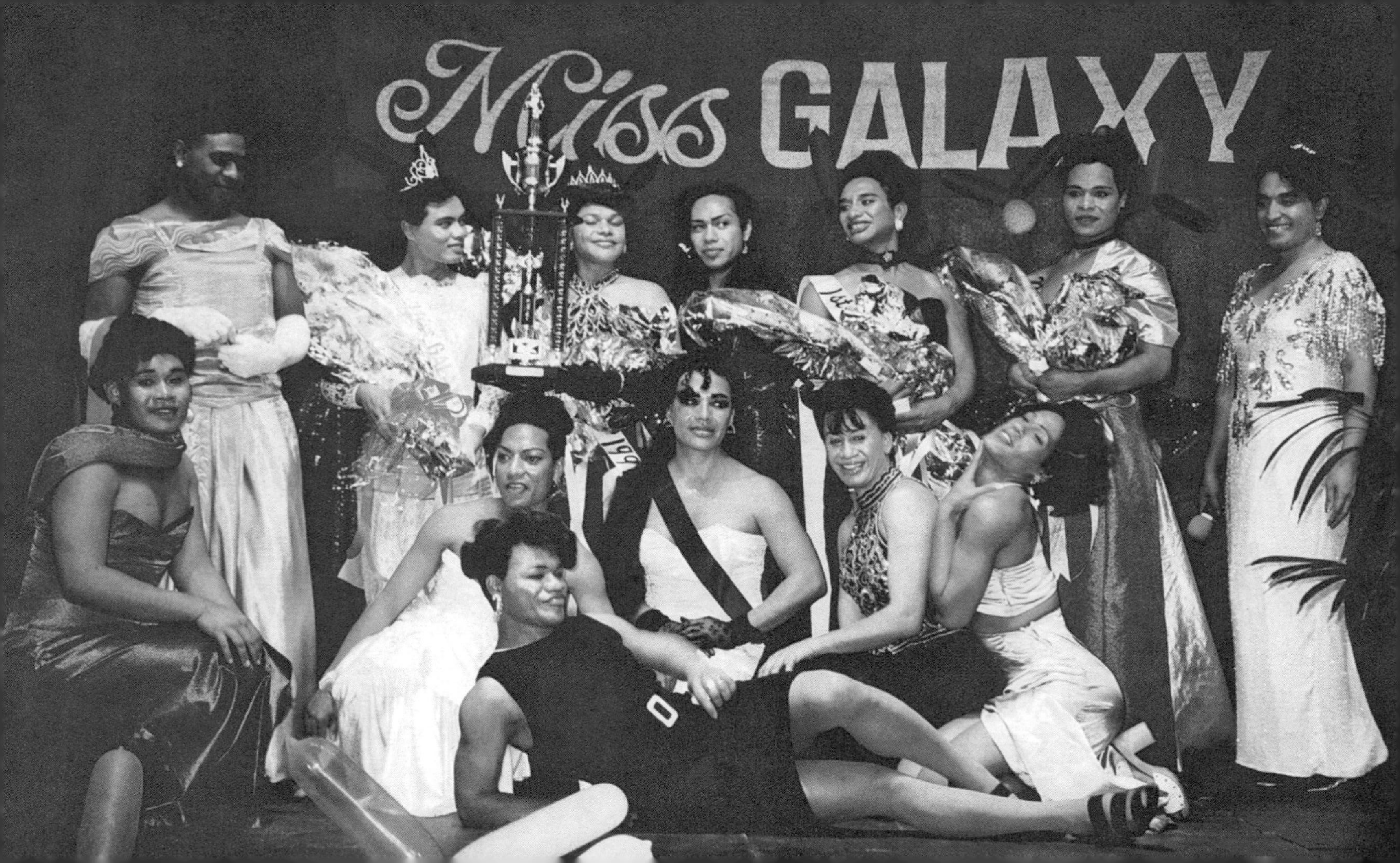
Miss GALAXY

cosmopolitan culture, about which the Tongan public is more ambivalent (Besnier 2011). Other contemporary performance arenas for Polynesian liminal males are also identified with tourist audiences, nightclub floor shows, and all-female gatherings, such as bridal showers (Mageo 1992).

The close association between performance, gender liminality, and reversals of the social order is widespread in Polynesia, and dancing, particularly, has a strong antistructural component. Dances mirror some of the oppositional elements and tensions in Polynesian society, including those between male and female, and between females as virginal "girls" and as mature, sexually active wives and mothers (Mageo 1992; Shore 1981). These elements contrast with the Polynesian emphasis on decorum, emotional restraint, and respect behavior, especially where brothers and sisters are present, and particularly apply to discussing or expressing sexual matters in gender-mixed company. The association of gender liminality in Polynesia with a lack of restraint and decorum, particularly regarding sexuality, makes gender liminal individuals particularly suitable for secular entertainments. Indeed, the sexually suggestive performances of, for example, the fa'afafine in contemporary Samoa suggest one explanation of their role: Where the virgin girl is still the cultural ideal, the "outrageous" behavior of the fa'afafine provides a negative role model of how girls should not behave. In traditional Samoa, these antistructural performances were in fact performed by girls who visited villages other than their own, where the males would not fall into the category of brothers. With the advent of Christianity, which is now thoroughly embedded as a source of Polynesian morality, these traditional elements of culture for the most part have been suppressed, and the norm-breaking nature of dance performances has to a large extent been taken over by the fa'afafine (Mageo 1992).

The transgender performances in Polynesia are particularly appropriate venues for the expression and display of transgender identity; they confirm an individual's femininity through transvestism; feminine accessorizing, such as wearing makeup, flowers, and perfume; creativity in composing songs; and dancing (Besnier 1996:297). In addition, cultural performances provide an important avenue of prestige and economic reward for gender liminal males, who are seriously marginalized in Polynesian society by their failure to play the important male roles of husband and father of many children. This failure puts them outside the serious arenas of politics and ceremonial activities around which prestige in Polynesia is centered (Besnier 1996). Only if the gender liminal abandons his gender nonconformity by marrying

Opposite page: Contestants in the 1997 Miss Galaxy beauty pageant pose around the proud winner and with the emcee. Beauty contests, associated with modernity and globalization, emphasize the importance of performing gender diversity in Polynesia. (Photograph © Niko Besnier.)

and becoming a household head can he participate as a meaningful male member of Polynesian society.

GENDER LIMINALITY AND THE POLYNESIAN CONCEPT OF THE PERSON

One significant factor that may explain the widespread role of transgender males is the Polynesian concept of the person. This concept focuses on the importance of the social role rather than on the individual as a holistic and atomistic entity, so central to modern Euro-American culture. In Polynesia, persons are made up of different aspects, including male and female, which are foregrounded in different social contexts. Thus, gender liminality, like other aspects of a person, is highly context dependent, viewed not as indicating a particular kind of person but rather as a relationship between an individual and a social context. Thus, as in much of Southeast Asia, there is a gap between the social importance given to what people do in public and what they do in private. Additionally, a person may be derided for some aspects of his or her character in some contexts, while praised for other aspects of his or her character or behavior in other contexts. Unlike American society, where an individual's total persona may be spoiled by one stigma (Goffman 1963), in Polynesia the "person" is a multifaceted identity, and occupying a gender liminal status is not the basis of a totalizing characterization.

In contrast to sex/gender variance among Native Americans and the ritualized homosexuality of some parts of neighboring Melanesia, neither of which "survived the moral onslaught of colonial authorities and missionaries," in Polynesia today gender diversity appears to be increasing (Besnier 1997). Whatever the traditional reasons for the emergence and maintenance of gender liminality in Polynesia, in contemporary Polynesian societies gender diversity is being realized in the contexts of the modification of traditional cultural patterns, such as the performances of fa'afafine at bridal showers, and also in entirely new patterns, such as the association of gender liminal men with foreigners in urban Polynesian bars for the purpose of sexual relations. As Besnier notes, one of the striking aspects of gender liminal persons in Polynesia is their association with innovation, their willingness to adapt, and their role in social change. In Polynesia, the gender liminal person has more than usual contact with foreigners and is frequently found in urban centers, engaged in occupations that involve him in a cash or even a global economy and in a new discourse of gender and sexuality. In this, as in other ways, he has much in common with the *kathoey* of Thailand and the *bakla* of the Philippines, discussed in the following chapter.

Review and Reflection

1. Explain the meaning of "gender liminal" and why this term is preferred by ethnographers in the Pacific for sex/gender diversity.

2. Give examples of three different diverse sex/gender roles in the Pacific and the criteria used to define them.

3. Analyze, from a Polynesian perspective, the difference between a māhū and a homosexual. Explain how these differences are being affected by Western influences.

4. Describe the responses of Western explorers to sexuality and gender diversity in Polynesia. In your judgment, were these responses positive, negative, or ambivalent; support your answer with examples.

5. Describe the varied responses, both traditional and contemporary, of Polynesian societies to gender liminal individuals.

6. Looking back: Using examples of cultural patterns such as cultural performance, religion, work roles, sexuality, concept of the individual, or others, compare gender liminal roles in the Pacific with those of Native Americans and hijras.

Chapter Five

Transgendered Males in Thailand and the Philippines

In contemporary Thailand the most widely used term for gender diversity is **kathoey**, which primarily refers to males who appropriate feminine attributes and behaviors, particularly transvestism. Because kathoey are somewhat negatively stigmatized as effeminate homosexuals, who are like women but are also not women, some transgendered men have chosen to identify themselves as *sao brophet song*, that is, "a second type of woman," or a biological male that has the soul of a woman (Costa and Matzner 2007:1).

Thailand's culture is closely associated with Theravada Buddhism, and much of what is known about Thai sex/gender diversity historically is based on Buddhist records. In Thai culture, biological sex, culturally ascribed gender, and sexuality are not clearly distinguished, and all are included in the Thai term *phet*. Historically, the Thai sex/gender system included an intermediate category, kathoey, which included both males and females and existed alongside normative masculine and feminine identities (Jackson 1997a, 1997b).

Thailand today contains multiple sex/gender discourses, and transgendered individuals experience variable and changing identities. In traditional Thai culture, sexual orientation and sexual practices were not the basis of a personal or social identity, and the modern Western opposition of homosexual/heterosexual as types of persons did not exist. Since the 1950s, however, Western biomedical concepts of homosexuality and, more recently, Western concepts of "gay" identity have become part of Thai culture.

Similar to the Philippines, contemporary Thai sex/gender diversity is significantly associated with beauty and stage performances. Much Western writing portrays Thailand as tolerating or even approving of sex/gender diversity, partly because it is highly visible both on stage and in the streets. In reality, however, Thai attitudes toward sex/gender diversity are complex and ambivalent and include hostility and ridicule. Sao brophet song narratives suggest that Thai acceptance or tolerance may be exaggerated, as many include incidences of discrimination and even physical violence (Costa and Matzner 2007). A more accurate characterization might be that Thai sex/gender diversity is accepted mainly at the margins of society, except in the entertainment and beauty industries. However, the energetic state regulation of sexuality in the West contrasts with the absence of such legislation in Thailand.

The overlay of Western culture and the absence or bias of historical records make it difficult to accurately reconstruct traditional Thai attitudes toward sex/gender diversity. It appears historically that transvestite, transgender, "third sexes," and other forms of sex/gender diversity were accommodated more easily than they are today, though it is not clear that there is any continuity between hermaphrodite figures in Thai creation myths and contemporary kathoey. In addition, in some parts of Thailand, the hermaphrodites described in some of these myths were regarded negatively (Costa and Matzner 2007:21). Homoeroticism, however, was unmarked and was not a matter for surveillance either by the Buddhist religion or state law.

Buddhist origin myths describe three original human sex/genders—male, female, and biological hermaphrodite or kathoey. The kathoey was *not* defined merely as a variant of male or female, but as an independently existing third sex, perhaps with a secondary meaning of a male who acts like a woman. This system of three human sexes, with the kathoey as the third sex, remained prevalent in Thailand until the mid-twentieth century.

In the 1950s, a Western "scientific" or biomedical discourse on sex and gender was introduced into Thailand. Its Thai version emphasized the difference between homosexuals, who were viewed derogatorily as psychological "inverts," and kathoey, who were viewed as biological hermaphrodites (Jackson 1997b:61). This biomedical approach implicitly continued older, Buddhist views that kathoey were natural phenomena whose condition was a result of karmic fate, preordained from birth and beyond their capacity to alter. This view is still commonly held in Thailand both by ordinary people and by kathoey. The identification of the biomedical with the Buddhist position preserved—indeed, was developed in part to preserve—the traditional Thai ethical position regarding kathoey: People who are different or disabled because of their karma should be pitied rather than ridiculed, and kathoey are not sinful because their behavior is beyond their control.

Traditionally, kathoey referred to biological hermaphrodites, but it now refers mainly to transgendered males. (Photograph by Ravinder Nanda.)

While the diffusion of the Western biomedical model negatively affected social attitudes toward sex/gender diversity (Garcia 1996; Jackson 1997b), the more recent incorporation of a Western-inspired "gay" identity puts a more favorable gloss on sex/gender nonconformity. Until the 1970s, males and females, (biological) hermaphrodites, and cross-dressing men and women all came under the umbrella term, "kathoey." Subsequently, however, "kathoey" was dropped for cross-dressing masculine females, who are now universally referred to as *tom*, derived from the English "tomboy." The feminine lesbian partners of the tom, previously not distinguished from gender-normative females, are called *dee* (from the last syllable of lady, see Morris 1994). As a result of these shifts the term "kathoey" is most commonly understood as a male transgender category, which in different contexts can also include transvestites (cross-dressers), hermaphrodites, transsexuals, and effeminate homosexuals (Jackson 1997b:60).

HOMOEROTICISM IN THAI CULTURE

Homosexual activity between masculine-identified men, called "playing with a friend" (and applied to lesbians as well), has historically been distinguished in Thailand from sex between a man and a

(feminine) kathoey, whose homoeroticism was viewed as rooted in biological hermaphroditism. The biomedical and the Buddhist views reinforce the popular Thai belief that cross-gender sexual relations (that is,
between a kathoey and a man) are less stigmatizing than same-gender
sexuality (between two masculine-appearing males), because men,
unlike kathoey, are not fated to engage in this type of activity. Same-
sex/gender eroticism (the homosexuality of the modern West) was considered inauspicious, resulting in natural disasters, such as droughts,
being struck dead by lightning, or becoming crazy. These consequences
do not appear to have been directed at (heterogender) man/kathoey
relationships (Jackson 1997b:63–64).

In traditional Thai sex/gender discourse, male (and female) homoeroticism was understood as sex/gender inversion or "psychological
hermaphroditism," that is, having a woman's mind in a man's body.
Though homoeroticism has long been recognized in Thailand, Thai culture and language did not recognize distinctive homosexual or heterosexual identities for those homoerotic males and females who in other
respects adhered to normative masculine or feminine gender roles.
Thus, traditionally, same-sex sexual orientation and erotic practices
were not central in defining the gender identities of man, woman, or
kathoey. However, this has now changed.

Echoing the Indian discourse about hijras, "genuine" hermaphroditic kathoey are distinguished from "false" or "artificial" kathoey, who
are transgendered homosexuals. This distinction continues to emphasize that the genuine kathoey has both male and female genitals.
Although the older definition of kathoey as a distinctive intermediate
or third sex/gender category (with no reference to sexuality) is still
sometimes used in the popular media, the dominant popular stereotype
of the kathoey today is that of a male who dresses and acts like a
woman and who sexually relates exclusively to other males (in the
receptor role) (Morris 1994; Jackson 1997a:312, fn 6). Some kathoey,
however, identify themselves as women, or having a woman's soul in a
man's body. In the last decades of the twentieth century, and continuing
to the present time, the biomedical definition of homosexuality as an
inversion became central in the cultural construction of the kathoey,
who is now primarily considered a transgendered homosexual rather
than a biological hermaphrodite (Jackson 1997a:172).

TRANSFORMATIONS IN
TRADITIONAL SEX/GENDER IDEOLOGY

In the 1970s, the term "gay" entered into Thailand, changing the
meanings of homoeroticism and kathoey and also changing the struc-

ture of Thai sex/gender diversity. In traditional Thailand male homo-eroticism was largely ignored if it remained private. As in Brazil, insertive anal sex by a masculine appearing man did not damage his masculine identity; indeed, it might be viewed as an enjoyment of sexual variety that was "natural" to Thai men and even enhanced masculine identity. "Feminine" sexual practices, specifically taking the receptor role in anal sex, were stigmatized and if publicly known, defined a man as socially deficient, ranking even lower than a kathoey.

When the English term "gay" entered Thai culture, it referred mainly to cross-dressing or effeminate homosexual males; by the 1990s, however, the Thai image of gay became increasingly masculinized (as also occurred in Euro-American culture by the 1960s). The gay man in Thailand today is identified with gym-enlarged biceps and pectoral muscles and with accentuated body and facial hair. As postings in various forms of media demonstrate, the Thai gay confidently proclaims his identity as a man (Jackson 1995).

Self-identified gay men in Thailand are equally or even more concerned with their masculine identity than heterosexual men and model themselves on the dominant masculine image except for their sexual orientation. This masculinized gay identity, which strongly disassociates itself from the imputed feminine gender status of the kathoey, is now well established among the educated and middle-classes and appears to be filtering down to the lower and working classes. Gay identity offers Thai males who engage in sex with men a new subjectivity; "gay" now exists alongside the category of kathoey, and both categories appear to be growing.

The emerging gay identity in Thailand blurs the earlier opposition between "masculine" and "feminine" roles in same-sex erotic practices in which the man penetrated the kathoey, never the reverse. In the new Thai construct of gay identity "insertive" and "receptive" anal sex no longer define gender roles but are viewed as mere personal preferences. Gay identity in Thailand today is thus identified with homoerotic preference (sexual orientation), *not* (as in Brazil) with any particular sexual practice (i.e., active vs. passive sex role). "The gay" (the term commonly used in Thailand) represents the emergence of a third term added to the earlier structure of Thai male sex/gender categories in which kathoey and man were positioned as polar opposites.

Gay identity may be relatively new in contemporary Thailand, but it refers to an earlier, implicit, subcategory of masculine status: a man who is gender normative in all but his homoerotic preferences. Gay identity is thus consistent with the traditional Thai concept of "man" as a sex/gender category that accommodated homoerotic preferences as simply a variation of masculine sexuality in men who otherwise were gender normative.

In today's Thai popular culture, the categories of man (which includes gays and heterosexual men) and kathoey are viewed as polar opposites: Each category represents a constellation of sexual norms and gender characteristics regarded as mutually exclusive. A Thai man regards himself as either a man or a kathoey. In the modern Thai sex/gender system the kathoey becomes the negative "other" against which the masculine identities of both gays and men are defined (Jackson 1997a:172). The Thai gay man defines himself as a man and not as a kathoey, rejecting all the kathoey's feminine attributes except his exclusive same-sex orientation. Together, gays, men, and kathoey form structurally related components of an emerging Thai sex/gender system: Each component defines and supports the construction of the other. With the emergence of "the gay" as a masculine identity, the kathoey's transgendered behavior and feminine gender identity, along with their inverted sexuality, become structurally significant, distinguishing them from other males.

The pluralistic sex/gender system in contemporary Thailand, then, includes a borrowed Western system of four sexualities (man/woman, homosexual/heterosexual), in which the homosexual/heterosexual binary crosses the man/woman binary (see Morris 1994), as well as a more culturally indigenous system of three sex/genders—kathoey, woman, and man. The older system has been transformed and adjusted by the diffusion of the newer, Western model and more changes may lie in the future.

SOCIAL ATTITUDES TOWARD THE KATHOEY

As in other patriarchal cultures, in Thailand the devalued status of women stigmatizes effeminate or transgendered men. The stigma attached to the kathoey today is reinforced by the contemporary denigration of transgendered homosexuality by self-identified gay males and the larger society. This suggests that it is not same-sex sexuality per se that is stigmatizing, but rather the associated mark of femininity. Both traditionally and currently, a Thai male who dresses, talks, and acts like a Thai man and who fulfills his social obligations by marrying and fathering a family is honored by being considered a man, even if his preferred sexual partner is a male.

As noted earlier, in traditional Thai culture, homoeroticism was neither condemned as sinful nor criminalized. Thai society is generally noninterventionist in sexual matters, and Thai culture (like much of Southeast Asia) puts a greater premium for everyone on the conventionality of one's public acts, rather than on the nonconformity of one's private emotions or behavior. Therefore, a homosexual orientation that does not publically breach masculine gender norms need not be—and is not viewed as—an inevitable source of confrontation with society or a matter of social condemnation. How one acts is more important than how one feels, and the public expression of one's "true self" is not valued in the same way as it is in the West (Morris 1994). Thus, "coming out" as a gay or a kathoey brings a "loss of face," because there is no compensating value to "being oneself." Against this Thai cultural pattern, the visibility of the kathoey becomes less rather than more valued.

Nonetheless, traditionally and also in some contemporary contexts, kathoey are "accepted." They are highly visible and found in all social strata (except at the highest levels of Thai nobility). Kathoey live and work openly in cities, rural towns, and villages. Many perform in transvestite revues at gay bars and theaters; kathoey transvestite beauty contests are very popular and attended by local dignitaries, politicians, the public at large, and tourists. Thai men and women exhibit an open fascination with kathoey (in contrast to the Indian attitude toward hijras, but similar to the attitude toward bakla in the Philippines), who are viewed as entertaining and humorous and are also associated with feminine grace, elegance, and beauty (Jackson 1997b:71).

Among upper-middle-class urbanites, however (again similar to the Philippines), kathoey are criticized for being loud, lewd, and vulgar, which is considered to be particularly un-Thai-like behavior. Although many kathoey work at ordinary jobs and also run their own businesses, they have the reputation of being sexual libertines and prostitutes, which contributes to their generally derided social position. In the past this sexual license was accepted in Thailand, possibly because the kathoey provided a "safe" sexual outlet for unmarried youth, whose sexual initiations might otherwise sully the reputation of young unmarried women (Jackson 1997a:173), a role similar to that played by transgendered males in the Philippines (Whitam 1992).

With the emergence of the gay as a masculine male and the changing meaning of kathoey from biological hermaphrodite to transgendered homosexual, however, kathoey face increasing social and sexual stigmatization, and even physical violence (Jackson 1997a:171). The kathoey's cross-gender persona, with its assumed permanent sexual subordination in the receptor role, now makes him a kind of "deficient male," not an independent sex/gender category. The kathoey is also derided because he rejects the strongly sanctioned expectation that all Thai men other than Buddhist monks should marry and become fathers. Furthermore, kathoey are increasingly derided because of their homosexuality, which, influenced by mid-twentieth-century American psychiatry and generally accepted in scientific/academic discourse and among the Thai upper-middle, educated classes, is viewed as a derogatory category that includes "inversion" and, therefore, "perversion."

By the 1970s and 1980s, transvestites and transsexuals were also distinguished from (biological) hermaphrodites and viewed as "false" kathoey, who, like homosexual men, were considered to suffer from a psychological disorder. Homosexuality and male transgenderism are now considered "social problems" by Thai academics and the upper-middle classes. Attempts to "root out" these "perversions" have become part of official rhetoric, which at the same time, however, urges compassion toward homosexuals and transgenderists as individuals.

The complex and multiple discourses regarding Thai sex/gender diversity belie Thailand's international reputation of being not just tolerant but welcoming of such diversity. This welcome, in fact, has an important economic basis, as the successful marketing of "pink chic" accounts for a substantial part of the Thai economy, which heavily depends on tourist dollars (Fuller 2013). Nevertheless, culture also counts: The echoes of a more humane and flexible past regarding sex/gender diversity in Thai culture continues to influence contemporary attitudes.

SEX/GENDER DIVERSITY IN THE PHILIPPINES

Gender roles in the indigenous, pre-Euro-American contact period in the Philippines, like other Southeast Asian cultures, were generally complementary and egalitarian (Peletz 2009). One's biological sex and sexual practices had little bearing on one's identity or social position and there was a long tradition of highly valued male transvestite and transgendered roles (Errington 1990; Garcia 1996). Ritual and healing roles were associated with feminine attributes and were occupied by females or transvestite males, called *babaylan*, who dressed and acted like women, which accorded them sacred power and prestige (Errington 1990; Garcia 1996:125ff). The homosexual relationships of these men were not culturally marked and were apparently irrelevant to transgendering for ritual purposes. As in Brazil, India, and some Native American cultures, the male sexual partner of the babaylan was considered a "normal" man.

In the complex state societies of island Southeast Asia, transgendered and cross-dressed males were associated with sacred personages, were guardians of state regalia, were ritual healers, and were accomplished singers and dancers who performed at various celebrations and rites of passage. Influenced by Hinduism, where the union of sex/gender opposites is a central religious theme, transvestites and transgendered figures were metaphors for cosmic unity. They embodied ancestral continuity and potency, mediating between a divine world and the mundane world of human beings (Johnson 1997:12, 25). Historically, then, gender diversity in the Philippines was not marginal in society but was symbolically central.

Unlike the relative continuity of Thai culture up to the present, however, the Philippines experienced transforming foreign domination, first by Muslim Arabs, later by Spain (from the sixteenth to the nineteenth centuries), and still later by United States occupation in 1898 as a result of the Spanish American war. An important cultural effect of this foreign domination was a "sexualizing" and masculinizing of Filipino culture: Women lost status and power to men; the Islamic ethic emphasized male potency and women as the embodiment of the pure and the traditional (Johnson 1997); the Catholic Spanish culture introduced the surveillance and denigration of homosexual relations, labeled sodomy and male transgendering; and, as in Thailand, an American scientific discourse defined homosexuality as a pathological inversion (Garcia 1996). Thus, external cultural impositions dominate Filipino concepts of sex/gender diversity today, though older traditions have not been completely eliminated and, indeed, are being revitalized.

CONTEMPORARY CONSTRUCTIONS OF GENDER DIVERSITY: TRANSGENDERED MALE HOMOSEXUALITY

Contemporary Filipino gender diversity centers on male trans-gender roles variously called *bakla, bantut, or bayot,* depending on the region. These roles conflate effeminacy in appearance and manner-isms, transvestism, psychic inversion, and same-sex sexual relations. Bakla are males with a feminine "heart" or spirit, who cross-dress and who are assumed to take the feminine (receptor) role in sex. As in Thai-land, Filipino sex/gender ideology traditionally did not include a homo-sexual/heterosexual distinction in which "homosexual" refers to both partners in a same-sex sexual relationship. Only the transgendered bakla, stereotyped as a "pseudo-woman," is considered homosexual (Manalansan IV 1995:197).

The term "bakla" has negative connotations of indecisive, weak, cowardly, vulgar and low-class—the screaming drag queen of the 1960s Stonewall rebellion (Manalansan IV 1997). The term "bantut" has even stronger negative connotations; used in Muslim areas of the Philip-pines, it denotes male impotence and a "joke of a woman," or more seri-ously, a defiled woman (in opposition to the purity of normal women). Bantut are neither man nor woman, and their receptor role in same-sex sexual relations is considered an abomination in Muslim culture (John-son 1997).

Like the opposition of man and kathoey in Thailand, in the Philip-pines a "real man" is "one who is not bakla": he is defined as "brave" and "level headed" and by his participation in family life (Garcia 1996:55). "Bakla" sometimes refers to a hermaphrodite or a physically deficient male, though there is no evidence that bakla are anatomically different from other men. Because of the negative connotations of local terms for gender diversity, many bakla prefer to self-identify as "gay," a term that carries a positive connotation of Western modernity and cosmopolitaness, which does not, as in Brazil, identify their masculine partners.

The bakla's core gender identity or "heart" is feminine, an identification based on the Filipino cultural concepts of "inside" (*loob*) and "outside" (*labas*). This binary distinction emphasizes that the identity of all individuals—man, woman, or other—is largely based on an inner, subjective reality (the loob), which guides, affirms, and dominates external appearance (the labas). The term "bayot," for example, literally translated as "a woman with a penis," privileges the inner reality of a woman's heart, spirit, or psyche against the outward appearance as a genital (anatomic) male (Garcia 1996, citing Hart, p. 55). This contrasts to an earlier Western conception of inversion that privileges the body as the standard against which the psychic opposition was viewed as "abnormal."

BAKLA SEXUAL RELATIONSHIPS

The same-sex sexual relations of the bakla is only one factor in socially defining his role, but it is very important in his subjective identity and its effect on public attitudes. Contrary to the Western categorical distinction between homosexuals and heterosexuals, there is frequent sexual interaction between bakla and nonbakla in the Philippines. It is reported that perhaps 75 percent of young, working-class boys and young adults, who later marry heterosexually, have sex for money with bakla (Whitam 1992). Referred to as "callboys," like the maridos of Brazilian travestís, these boys are not socially marked as homosexuals and do not experience themselves as such. The Filipino view that only the "feminine" partner in the sexual relationship is a homosexual reinforces the emphasis on the feminine loob as the core of bakla identity.

Masculine-appearing men, who are assumed to take the inserter sexual position, are also assumed to have a masculine loob; they are thus real men even as they have sexual relations with bakla. In spite of the fact that callboys or male partners of bakla acknowledge sexual satisfaction as well as monetary benefits from their bakla relationships, the masculine-appearing partner stoutly denies any deep affection or emotional impact in the relationship; only the feminine bakla is publically viewed as deeply emotionally affected by these sexual relationships.

Both Western and Filipino biomedical views of inversion presume that only one partner in a homosexual relationship is an invert; thus, as in Thailand, in the Philippines it is the transgendered male who is assumed also to play the "feminine" or receptor role in sex, who has become "the homosexual." Like Brazilian travestís, Filipino bakla say that to penetrate a man transforms the penetrated man into a woman. They explicitly reject the possibility that they could accept a man who wishes to be penetrated by them as their boyfriend. Among the bakla, then, as in society at large, a man who desires penetration loses his masculine identity.

Bakla conform to the "heterogender" nature of sexual relationships dominant in the Philippines and insist that sexual relations between two bakla is repulsive and never occurs. In some regions of the Philippines, two bayot having sex with each other is considered "incest" or "eating their own flesh" (Garcia 1996:97). Emphasizing the heterogender nature of their sexual relations, many bakla define the core of their feminine identity as their exclusive sexual and romantic interests in "real" men, or as women who wish to be penetrated by a "real" man (Johnson 1997:90). Similar to some Brazilian travestís, some bakla say that their first experience of anal penetration, however violently imposed, confirmed their transgendered identity in their own eyes (Johnson 1997).

Bakla typically express their desire for a real man as deep longing; they experience themselves as having the "weaker" emotions of women, an image based on sexual desire as shaped by the gender hierarchy and the view that women, like the Virgin Mary (a powerful image in Catholic Filipino culture), were meant to suffer for men. This imitation of the stereotypical female in a patriarchal culture is at the core of the bakla role (Manalansan IV 1995:197). Bakla acknowledge that however sexually desirable they are, the mutuality of their relationships with real men are limited because bakla cannot bear children. Thus, they feel doomed to suffer in their love relationships no matter how feminine and subservient they are (Cannell 1995:241).

Yet, paradoxically, bakla, like hijras, travestís, and some Polynesian gender variants, are also are viewed as sexual aggressors. And, as in these cultures, the material benefits the bakla confer on their partners also give them a certain leverage and source of control in these relationships (Manalansan IV, personal communication 1999). Thus, bakla, like travestís, hijras, māhū, and Indonesian waria, are by no means merely victims in unequal sexual relationships.

THE ASSOCIATION OF
TRANSGENDERED MALES WITH BEAUTY

Beauty in the Philippines is associated with successful performance, which essentially includes the ability to transform oneself convincingly from one's ordinary role. The aim is less to "pass" as what one is not than to act convincingly in a temporary role through dress and other behavioral appropriations. The bakla, as males who display a highly successful ability to present themselves as women within certain contexts, are therefore closely associated with the concept of beauty in their own eyes and in the eyes of society (Cannell 1995:242; 1999). This transformative ability is expressed in their specialized occupations in fashion, entertainment, hairstyling, and beauty salons and particularly in their participation in beauty contests.

Bakla identity, formed around the "inside/outside structure" of the loob and the labas, calls for the loob—the inside female spirit—to be "exposed" by inscribing feminine beauty on the body, the most concrete site of the expression of the loob (Johnson 1997:90). Bakla beauty is understood as bodily practices aimed at style, glamour, and femininity. In defining themselves as feminine, bakla/bantut emphasize the care they give their bodies: their concern with cleanliness and beauty; their use of facial creams and body lotion to "soften" their bodies; their wearing of makeup, jewelry, and perfume; and their cross-dressing (Johnson 1997). The importance of beauty to transgendered identities emerges in bantut life-histories, particularly in the notion of "exposure" (Johnson 1997:124). For many bantut, "coming out," which usually occurs in high school or college, is expressed as "exposing my beauty." Bantut commonly greet each other by asking, "How is your beauty?" instead of "How are you?" This emphasis on bodily appearance is consistent with the Philippine cultural understanding of the body as an important site for self-transformation. Thus, the bantut are not merely imitating women but are "capturing" the power of femininity through beautifying their bodies and through their gender transformations.

TRANSVESTITE BEAUTY CONTESTS

In Filipino culture, various kinds of transformations are associated with power (Cannell 1995, 1999). Positive social attitudes toward bakla are largely based on their ability to transform themselves into glamorous and stylish women. The most visible and compelling sites for the presentation of transgendered beauty are transvestite beauty contests, which are a growing phenomenon in Southeast Asia and the Pacific (Cohen et al. 1996; Besnier 2011). In transvestite beauty contests, bakla convey a highly valued, global, and cosmopolitan image of glamour and style identified with the West, particularly America, and associated in the Philippines with the upper-class, educated elite and celebrities, themselves shaped by Western culture.

Beauty contests give status and pleasure to the bakla, some of whom have an obsession with participating as a way of "exposing" their beauty. Most of the contests are organized around international themes, illustrated by names like Miss Gay World or Miss Gay International, which emphasize bakla identification with the powerful global "otherness" of America (Cannell 1995). This is reminiscent of the "Miss Galaxy" contest in Tonga, whose very name indicates its global aura, but which also, unlike the mainstream Tonga beauty contest, is conducted in English. The Filipino beauty contests may even be viewed as a reemergence of traditional ritual transvestite roles as mediating figures, though today instead of mediating between the divine and the mundane, the bakla mediate between the local and global culture (Cannell 1999; Johnson 1996:90; Peacock 1987).

Points in the beauty contests are awarded for beauty, such as "Best in Evening Gown" and "Miss Photogenic," but more than half the points are based on "intelligence," exemplified in the question-and-answer portion of the contest. The questions, which are asked and must be answered in English, relate to topics like politics and careers (Johnson 1996), again emphasizing a cosmopolitan, Western source of prestige. Though the material rewards of winning the contest are small, contestants take the contests very seriously. There is also an underlying comic tension; while the audience applauds genuine intelligence and beauty, there are also catcalls and glee when the "beauty" becomes unglued, as in a broken heel or a slippage of costume. Most contestants wear very tight underwear and full length stockings. They tape or tie their genitals between their thighs, and there is always anticipation that the male will emerge accidentally from the female, an occasion for laughter that is not always compassionate. The audiences for these contests are mainly nonbakla and include local dignitaries, village businesspeople, members of elite local families; men, women and children all attend.

The Americanized images of beauty in the contests are closely linked to the early-twentieth-century American colonial regime, which emphasized American-style education aimed particularly at transforming Filipinos into participating citizens of a modern, democratic state. Today, schools and educators are among the predominant sponsors not only of the beauty contests (which are mostly organized by bakla) but of the many other contests and performances (such as talent shows and sports events) that are part of American civic culture, which emphasizes discipline, self-development, and self-respect. As the question-and-answer portion of the beauty contests most clearly demonstrates, beauty is significantly about education, mastery of English, good citizenship, a professional career orientation, and democratic fair play, as well as glamour. In short, "beauty" is articulated by and associated with those institutions identified with the "knowledge power" of Americans, and beauty is a primary idiom within which this "global other" is identified.

Although generally the association of bakla with this international concept of beauty is a source of approval, in the Muslim areas of the south, the bantut identification with the global "other" generates ambivalence. The Muslims continually and actively resisted both Spanish and American domination; in this context, the core of the Muslim masculine ideal was an aggressive militarism that opposed external domination and stressed the feminine ideal of sexual purity. Thus, in Muslim-dominated areas, bantut are not only gender "deviants" but also cultural deviants. Bantut's identification with a globalized external culture, as well as with the Christianized Filipino state, lowers their status in Muslim areas. The positively valued "exposure" of bantut beauty turns into negatively valued "overexposure" (to the West) and undermines bantut acceptance in local communities (Johnson 1997).

During the 1970s, bakla unsuccessfully attempted to improve their social position by identifying themselves as a "third" sex/gender (*sward*) in an attempt to "naturalize" their sex/gender nonconformity and make it "equal" to that of men and women (Garcia 1996:197). But because homosexual relations in the Philippines are understood as heterogender, not homosexual, the idea of "thirdness" had little impact on bakla social status and perhaps confirmed rather than undermined the Filipino binary sex/gender system.

Still another context for understanding bakla identities is the migration of bakla to the United States. Anthropologist Martin Manalansan's (2003) ethnography of bakla, mostly in New York City, demonstrates the complex impact of globalization on the personal identities of gender variant individuals. He notes that the femininity, emphasis on beauty, and valuation of gender as a dramatic presentation associated with the bakla role in the Philippines remain important in their identities and their lives. But this "drag" identity not only marginalizes them in the masculine culture of the gay community in America, it also undermines their social status within that community. In addition, the folk Catholicism and the importance of family in the Philippines, which persists to some extent in the US diaspora, are cultural patterns that act as obstacles to bakla integration in the American urban gay milieu. At the same time, however, their ethnic identification serves as a positive bond within the immigrant community.

Review and Reflection

1. Discuss several ways in which Western ideas have affected ideas about gender diversity in Thailand.

2. Describe the historical and contemporary positions of Thai society on the gender diverse role of kathoey (sao brophet song), including the changes that occurred from early Buddhism to the present.

3. Thailand has been defined in the West as a "tolerant" society regarding sex/gender diversity. Do you agree or disagree with this statement; support your position with examples from the chapter.

4. Explain the meaning of "gay" and "tomboy" in contemporary Thai society. How do these terms identify different kinds of identities and how are they similar or different from their meanings in the West?

5. Describe how foreign domination and occupation influenced ideas about gender diversity in the Philippines.

6. Summarize the characteristics of "bakla" and explain how the role is related to concepts of "loob" and "labas."

7. Discuss the importance of beauty to bakla identity and behavior.

8. Looking back and looking forward: Explain the relationship of the beauty contest to gender diversity in Polynesia, Thailand, the Philippines, and Indonesia.

Chapter Six

Indonesia
Bissu, Waria, and Lesbi

Indonesia, a multiethnic island nation, shares some important cultural patterns with other nations in Southeast Asia, such as Thailand, the Philippines, and Malaysia, although there are also important differences. As noted earlier, historically Southeast Asia has been relatively accommodating of sex/gender diversity, due partly to the influence of Hindu religion and culture (Peletz 2009; Boellstorff 2005a). Sex/gender diversity in Indonesia has also been affected by the period of Dutch colonialism, political developments in the postcolonial Indonesian state, the variable nature of Islamic influence, and contemporary aspects of globalization (Davies 2010; Peletz 2009:13; Boellstorff 2005a:16–17; Blackwood 2005).

In addition to Islam other factors such as social class, family and kinship patterns, political structures, history, ethnic identities, and individual variation significantly affect contemporary Indonesia's attitudes toward sex/gender diversity. Prior to the arrival of Islam in the thirteenth century and Dutch colonialism and Christianity in the sixteenth century, a tolerant and even positively valued view of sex/gender diversity was allied with relative gender equality. Sacred powers of both male and female mixed gender individuals were highly valued, and space was permitted for a variety of erotic behaviors. Same-sex desires and relationships were often invisible or ignored and were not considered central to personal identity or a particular threat to society or culture.

These cultural patterns were undermined by Dutch colonialism and Christianity, the emergence of the "modern" postcolonial state, and, today, the increasing influence of conservative Islam. All these factors led to an increase in the surveillance and repression of sex/gender diversity in the twentieth century (see Blackwood 2005; Davies 2010). In the past 30 years the relation of the state to sex/gender diversity has again changed, leading to both the revitalization of traditional alternative sex/ gender roles and the emergence of new sex/gender identities, three of which—bissu, waria, and gay/lesbis—are described below.

Modern Indonesia contains over 300 distinct ethnic groups, over 700 distinct languages and dialects, and six officially recognized religions: Islam, Hinduism, Buddhism, Protestantism, Roman Catholicism, and Konghuchu, a form of Indonesian Confucianism. The Indonesian constitution stipulates freedom of religion, but citizenship is dependent on belonging to an officially recognized religion. Hinduism arrived in Indonesia in the eighth century; although today it is dominant only in Bali, elements of Hindu mythology and culture, such as the popular Ramayana shadow puppet plays, were absorbed into Indonesian court and contemporary popular culture. From the thirteenth through the fifteenth centuries, Islam, brought by traders, grew steadily in Indonesia though pre-Islamic beliefs and rituals still retain some influence. Although Islam is not the official religion of Indonesia, its interpretations, principles, and practices dominate the activities of the state, the lives of most of its citizens, and the construction and treatment of nonnormative gender roles and sexuality. Similar to other world religions, the relations between Islam, the state, and sex/gender diversity have varied over time and place (Murray and Roscoe 1995; Hossain 2012b; Boellstorff 2005b) and vary today within Indonesia as well (Davies 2010).

Local ethnic identity remains as important in Indonesia today as it was in precolonial and colonial times, but today Indonesian nationalism is strong and widespread, energetically fostered by the postcolonial governments. When Indonesia became an independent nation in 1945, its first president, Sukarno, in the face of communist resistance, mass Islamic and ethnic separatist movements, and conflicts in the military, made the creation of a national Indonesian identity one of his main goals (Boellstorff 2005a). In 1967, economic and political crises culminated in a violent political coup when Major General Soeharto seized power and promoted a "New Order" government, emphasizing modernity, economic development and globalization but also extending Sukarno's principle of national unity as a primary goal.

Soeharto (who was in power until 1998) promoted his "New Order" ideology through the "family principle," which stressed the importance of heterosexual marriage for all citizens, with a corresponding emphasis on normative sex/gender roles and the importance of reproduction (Davies 2007:45). Kinship and the family are central in Indonesian culture and are as strongly supported by the national government and by Islam as they had been by the Dutch. Both the colonial and postcolonial governments emphasized a strict patriarchal family structure, which severely undermined both the gender equality and the sex/gender diversity that had previously characterized much of Southeast Asia (Peletz 2009).

Today, under President Yudhoyono, Indonesian women are defined almost entirely in terms of being wives and mothers, subordinate to their husbands (Davies 2007:41). Marriage is even more important for women than for men; a woman who does not marry and have children will not automatically be granted full Indonesian citizenship (Blackwood 2005). Men are expected to be the family's primary income earner, make the important decisions affecting the family's best interests, and exclusively represent the family in public. Under Soeharto's rule, Indonesian civil servants, defined as representing the state and a symbol of its morality, were required to be heterosexually married. This pressure for normative sex and gender role conformity is expressed in the mass media, school curricula, social services, official festivities, and other public activities, though recent ethnography documents that sexuality in Indonesia is more complicated than official state ideology acknowledges (Bennett and Davies 2014).

The "family values" orientation of both Indonesian culture and Islam converges with the importance of honor and shame in Indonesian social relationships: Both sex/gender normative and nonnormative Indonesians are constantly alert to behaving in ways that do not bring shame on their families. This concern is consistent with the Indonesian (and Southeast Asian) value on the importance of the public presentation of self, which is aimed at sustaining harmony and consensus in social relations, in contrast to the Western value of expressing one's "true self," which can cause conflict with others (Wieringa 2008). Because women, particularly, embody a family's honor and are considered more emotional than men, their sexuality and their behavior are more closely watched. This Indonesian cultural pattern strongly affects the expression of sex/gender diversity, though in complicated and paradoxical ways. While the "New Order" regime and subsequent political policies have promoted the important contributions of bissu and waria to the Indonesian nation, this policy is not extended to gays and lesbians.

BISSU

Bissu, defined as androgynous shamans, have a long history among the Bugis, the largest ethnic group in South Sulawesi, Indonesia (Davies 2007; Boellstorff 2005a:40). Bissu combine features of both masculine and feminine gender roles: Historical evidence describes both phenotypical male and phenotypical female bissu, although today bissu are mainly males (Blackwood 2005:854; Peletz 2009:144; Boell-storff 2005a). The Bugis believe that bissu brought the first life to Earth and facilitated the first marriage, which partly explains their important role today in Indonesian weddings. Historically, bissu also were guardians of the sacred regalia of royal courts and protected the nobility.

Bissu power primarily involves the ability to contact the sacred realm of the divine through possession trance, which gives them the power to heal and to bestow blessings. There is a widespread traditional Southeast Asian belief that male and female were not separated in the origin of the world, and after the sexes became separated it was the bissu, who symbolically embody a perfect combination of male and female elements, that brought the sexes together again (Peletz 2009). Bissu describe their dual gender characteristics in various ways: One bissu described himself to anthropologist Sharyn Davies as being male on his right side, symbolized by the whiskers that grow only on the right side of his face; when he combines male and female dress, as bissu generally do, he wears flowers on his left, or female side (Davies 2007:89). The bissu ideal, like that of the Indian hijra, is an ascetic who should refrain from sex and repress sexual desire and other earthly pleasures. Based on this ideal, bissu are an exception to the rule that all men should get married. Some bissu even say that a bissu should not have a penis, or if a bissu has one, it should not be allowed to become erect. Yet, historically, bissu were known to have sexual relations with normative men, who they sometimes took as their "husband" (Peletz 2009:144). Even today, bissu are known to engage in sexual relations with "normal" men, though public knowledge of this detracts from a bissu's legitimacy.

There are several paths to becoming a bissu: Few bissu are in fact hermaphrodites, though biological intersexuality may be interpreted as a calling to become a bissu. Although bissu are known to have sex with (normal) men, homosexual desires are not part of a bissu's calling or identity. This calling may come in a dream, in which the potential bissu learns the special bissu language, but whatever the source of his calling, a publically acknowledged bissu must undergo certain rites of passage and training in order to access the knowledge and magic associated with being bissu. A bissu must learn special ritual dances, chants, and prayers, and he must become familiar with sacred bissu texts. In a final rite of passage, a bissu undergoes possession trance and is placed on a raft that is launched on a river. The bissu's spirit rises to heaven, and only if he is a real bissu, will he return from this journey, blessed by the spirit world.

Islamic, Dutch, and postcolonial governments necessitated some important transformations in the bissu role (Davies 2007). In 1957 when the power of local Indonesian kingdoms was replaced by a centralized national government, an important source of bissu prestige,

Bissu are traditional shamans who bless people for good health and successful journeys and play particularly important ritual roles in weddings. Bissu now play an important part in the cultural revitalization of Indonesia. (Photograph by Sharyn Graham Davies.)

connected to their association with royalty, declined. In addition, an emerging militant Muslim movement condemned bissu as anti-Islamic, characterizing bissu spirit possession as polytheism (the belief in many gods), which is incompatible with the Muslim belief in the oneness of Allah. This Islamic movement considered bissu identity and rituals shameful and sinful: During this period bissu were violently persecuted, punished, and even murdered; their sacred paraphernalia was thrown into the ocean; and their rituals could only be conducted secretly (Davies 2007:92). This repression continued under President Soeharto's New Order government, when bissu were considered both anti-Islamic and culturally "backward."

In 1998, however, when President Soeharto's government lost power, a general revitalization of traditional Indonesian culture (*adat*) was supported by subsequent reform governments. This led to new, although transformed roles for bissu, who now participated in rituals for ordinary people and were hailed as part of adat. In this capacity bissu were also "repackaged" as a tourist attraction (Boellstorff 2005a:40). Today, bissu grant blessings for good harvests and agricultural festivals, invoke protection against natural disasters, bless people before they undertake a journey, and give blessings to heal the sick.

Bissu officiate at life-cycle ceremonies, such as births and deaths, and have a particularly important role in weddings (see below). Bissu bless families for fertility, help with pregnancies, and bless newborn babies for strength and health. Bissu also bless houses and give advice on auspicious dates to begin construction. The efficacy of these blessings all depend on bissu spirit possession, a condition bissu prove by safely walking over hot coals, swallowing sharp knives, and walking through fire. At the height of the possession trance, a bissu forces his knife (*keris*) into his eyes, neck, stomach and other parts of his body, and the proof of his divine nature is that the knife does not penetrate his skin (Davies 2007: 96).

Contemporary Indonesian governments support the revitalization of Indonesian culture, and today bissu practices are not viewed as competing with or undermining Islam, but rather they are regarded as a fruitful melding between the two (Davies 2010). Bissu, for example, participate in important public Islamic rituals like male (and female) circumcision: Bissu organize the ceremony, give people instructions to carry out the ritual correctly, arrange the ritual food, and recite ritual blessings (Davies 2007:95). Bissu also bless people for a safe pilgrimage to Mecca (hajj), and indeed some bissu go on hajj themselves, an event officially recognized by the government (Davies 2010).

Bissu have key roles in Bugis weddings, especially among the elite, which includes wedding preparation and all wedding rituals. Upon arrival at the wedding site the groom and his entourage are led toward the house where the wedding will take place. Before the actual ceremony, the groom must overcome a series of ritual obstacles; in one of these the bissu interrogates him in the sacred bissu language to determine if his social status is consistent with that of the bride's family. After the groom successfully overcomes all the obstacles, the bissu leads him into the house for the wedding ceremony.

Based on his esoteric knowledge, only the bissu prepares the offerings to the deity; the bissu sits near the bride at the prayer reading; and only the bissu may seek divine blessings for the couple's fertility, which precedes any official Bugis marriage ceremony. In a final wedding ritual, the bissu performs a chant, after which the official marriage ceremony takes place (Davies 2007:113). These many ritual roles of the bissu illustrate one of the most prominent elements of the (transformed) revival of sex/gender diversity in Indonesia.

WARIA

Waria are biological males who express themselves as women in their dress, their comportment, their feminine hair styles, their exclu-

sive sexual desires for heterosexual men, and their rejection of heterosexual marriage. Some ethnographers as well as some waria
characterize waria, like bissu, as an alternative or "third" gender (Magerl 2000; Davies 2007; Oetomo 1996, 2000), while others consider them
an example of "male femininity," or male transvestites. Tom Boellstorff
notes, for example, the public toilets at waria performances are labeled
"women" and "man/waria," (2004a:161), a designation that some waria
have demanded (with limited success) on their national identity cards.

The term "waria," which is a composite of *wanita* (woman) *and*
pria (man), originated in a 1978 government dictate, aimed at replac-
ing the more derogatory, but still widely used term, *banci* (among the
Bugis they are called *calabai* [Davies 2007:45]). In the nineteenth century waria were mistakenly identified as hermaphrodites; they mainly
worked as low-class commodity traders around the city docks, as performers in low-class popular entertainments, known as *ludruk* (Peacock 1987), and as prostitutes. Because they were highly stigmatized,
waria/banci lowered their public profile by dressing as men in the day-
time. Today, waria almost universally, consistently, and publically
enact feminine roles, though, similar to some hijras, these are frequently exaggerations of normative feminine behavior, and when the
occasion demands it, waria may also exhibit rude and aggressive
behavior associated with men (Magerl 2000).

After Indonesian independence waria seemed to disappear from
public places, but like bissu, reemerged during Soeharto's regime. In
the late 1960s, though many waria were still prostitutes, many also
had become beauty salon workers, recognized for their expertise in
making up brides—and grooms—for their weddings. Waria also have
(limited) roles in wedding rituals for ordinary people, mainly organizing the food and dressing the bride.

Consistent with the goal of building national unity, Soeharto and
subsequent reform governments promoted public recognition of waria
as "human beings and as citizens of the nation," emphasizing the important contribution of waria beauty salon work to a national Indonesian
culture (Boellstorff 2004a). In 1972 the mayor of Jakarta, who saw
waria as being denied "a right to exist," supported the creation of a waria
association and tried to persuade the Indonesian public that waria
"played important roles in the Indonesian nation." Although in contrast
to bissu, waria are not viewed as part of traditional Indonesian culture,
their work in bridal beauty salons is an important source of their
income, prestige, government support, and sense of national belonging.

Waria also have important cultural roles in organizing public
entertainments, for example, waria playback singing (lip-syncing to
prerecorded music, both Western and local) and beauty contests, which
are supported by the government and attract wide segments of the pub-

Like the participants in the Miss Galaxy beauty contest in Tonga, the waria of Indonesia (called *calabaí* in Bugis) also represent international influences, producing innovative, Western-oriented fashions, elaborate hairstyles, and "campy" behavior, mostly in fashion parades. (Photograph by Sharyn Graham Davies.)

lic from all ethnic groups and social classes (Boellstorff 2004a). These performances enable waria to publically present their feminine selves in the context of promoting the ideology of national belonging. Waria also frequently appear in television sitcoms, music videos, commercial advertisements, and print media. They are also familiar figures in politics, performing at political party rallies, expressing preferences for candidates, and occasionally running for political office.

Waria who own beauty salons may become wealthy and are typically accepted as waria in their urban neighborhoods. Most waria are poor, however, as they are excluded from civil service and other regular jobs if they wear women's clothing. In some major cities, waria organizations, along with international and government-sponsored NGOs, (nongovernmental organizations) provide waria with various social services, help train waria in salon work, and promote health education, particularly aimed at preventing the spread of AIDS (Magerl 2000; Peletz (2009).

Almost all waria are self-declared Muslims and regularly perform Muslim rituals; some also go on hajj, which they must do as men. Many waria are acutely aware of the conflict between Islam and their commitment to femininity (Boellstorff 2005b), though Indonesian Islam itself is not uniformly conservative (Davies 2010). In any case, many waria try to mitigate the "sin" of their feminine identity and behavior by "doing good deeds" for their families and for the nation (Magerl 2000:27).

Waria generally reject homosexual desire as their motivation for becoming waria. They, like Bangladeshi hijras, differentiate themselves from "gay" men, by seeking only heterosexual male partners, whether as prostitutes or in longer-term relationships; unlike gays, they see their relationships as heterogenderal not homosexual. In contrast to gay men, waria experience their rejection of masculinity and their desire for femininity in their childhood or early teenage years, dismissing any interest in sports and preferring to play with girls. Waria almost universally find themselves in conflict with their families and may be harassed or even severely beaten. Because today various forms of male femininity may be defined as an illness, as well as a sin, the parents of some waria may take them to a professional psychologist to be "cured" (Peletz 2009:146). Waria refusal to marry is an important source of alienation from their families, though their families may eventually release them from this obligation. Some waria reconnect with their families later in life, but few feel they can act or dress as women in their home villages. This accounts for their running away to the cities, or even migrating to Europe (Noor 2012; see below).

In expressing their waria identity, some waria say they originate in the category "man" but have the soul and temperament of a woman; others say it is the way God made them; still others say it is their fate. Many waria undertake bodily modification by having silicone injections and taking massive doses of female hormone pills to enlarge their breasts, but few undergo sex-change operations, partly because of the expense and partly because they feel they must remain the sex God made them (Boellstorff 2004a:171). For waria, genital alteration is not central to being waria, as it is for hijras.

Waria explain that their public feminine gender role is an attempt to bring their body into alignment with their "soul." As ethnographer Tom Boellstorff aptly notes, waria have a performative sense of (their feminine) gender that must be worked at, which seems ideally suited for their beauty salon work where they transform the appearances of others (2004a:178).

Waria, like Bangladesh hijra, understand their sexual desires for men as the heterosexual desire of femininity for masculinity, an important distinction they make between themselves and gay men, who are identified as "desiring the same." While some Indonesians believe waria are genitally deformed or sexually impotent, most people understand, as do waria themselves, that waria desire and engage in sex with men, taking the receptive position mainly in oral sex (though sometimes in anal sex as well), for the pleasure it affords. Waria sexual partners are "normal" men who do not identify as gay (similar to India,

Bangladesh and Brazil), but rather may describe themselves as having a "passion for the feminine."

Like hijras, waria seek long-term romance with boyfriends or husbands who typically identify as normal and are accepted as such by their waria partners. Also, like Indian hijras, waria have an important hold on their male partners by financially supporting them, contrary to the normal man's role in the family (see Magerl 2000:65). In return, waria seek love and affection and are especially pleased if their boyfriends are affectionate in public. While many waria lose their boyfriends to heterosexual marriages, they may continue the relationship secretly.

Waria identity is primarily part of a local or national Indonesian culture, though more recently, waria connect to a global culture through the Internet. Waria are distinguished from Indonesian gays not only by their exclusive attraction toward heterosexual men, but also because of social class differences: In Indonesia a gay identity is more characteristic of the middle and upper classes, while waria are mainly working or lower class, at least in origin (Oetomo 1996:264). Although acknowledged for their cultural contributions in beauty salons and public performances, waria are ambivalently regarded in Indonesia, both because of increasing Islamic hostility toward homosexuality and their rejection of marriage. Thus, hundreds, perhaps even thousands of waria (and gay Indonesian men) have migrated to Europe (Noor 2012:3).

Through in-depth ethnography and oral narratives, Basittanti Noor has explored the diverse ways in which waria (and gay Indonesians) negotiate their sexual and romantic relationships with European men in Belgium and the Netherlands (2012). These relationships, involving individuals from very different cultures, require adjustment on both sides in relation to issues of social class; domestic and economic roles within the relationship; association with religion, both Islam and Christianity; connections between waria and their Indonesian families; age differences; lifestyle; and individual temperament.

Central to Noor's analysis are the fantasies that waria and Western men have about each other, which she sees as extensions of the historical "orientalist" stereotyping of the "other" that Europeans have applied to Middle Eastern cultures. European men fantasize about Indonesians as warm, submissive, graceful, slim-bodied, dark-skinned, and exotic; waria have a reverse "occidentalist" fantasy and are attracted by the muscular bodies, blue eyes, fair skin, and also the wealth of Europeans.

Waria in the Netherlands elaborate their femininity through wearing brand-name clothing, applying makeup, and using feminine gestures in order to attract European men both as short-term and long-term sexual partners. While traditional Indonesian mythology does include some nuanced references to "romantic love" (Wieringa 2008), waria in both Indonesia and Europe mainly learn about "romance" through Western media, especially movies and romance novels, and say they experience romantic love only in their relationships with Western men.

These romantic fantasies, however, are often disrupted by the practical realities of culture conflict and the absence of a wide range of common interests and values (Noor 2012:51). A common difficulty waria face is balancing a commitment to their present relationships in Europe with a commitment to their families in Indonesia. A waria may try to mitigate his family's rejection by sending money back home, though this can become a burden, especially if he is economically dependent on his European partner. The immigrant waria's rejection of heterosexual marriage and having children may result in guilt feelings (as it also does for waria living in Indonesia). Some waria contemplate a return to Indonesia and heterosexual marriage in the future to absolve these guilt feelings.

Difficulties in intimate waria/European relationships are also exacerbated by age differences. For example, Dutch men are typically 15–20 years older than their waria partners, and many—though not all—do not share the younger partner's interest in going to parties and "having adventures" (Noor 2012:52).

In the separation from their families and immersion in the foreign culture of the Netherlands, many waria, even those in intimate relationships with European men, experience deep loneliness. In response, some reinvigorate their commitment to Islam through participating in religious rituals and communal religious groups (Noor 2012:6). But even this may present difficulties, as today in Europe, and increasingly in Indonesia, contemporary Islam is becoming more outspoken in its rejection of "homosexuality" as being incompatible with Islam. Thus, pain and guilt remain; though for some waria, religious participation does create a sense of belonging otherwise absent in their lives (Noor 2012:47).

In addition, although European secularism encourages a personal freedom highly valued in the West, secularism and individualism, like other aspects of modernity, contrast strongly with traditional Indonesian culture and may be a source of great anxiety (Noor 2012:42; also see Besnier 2010). Also, paradoxically, waria feel threatened by the increasing anti-Islamic attitudes in Europe. Unlike the emerging gay/lesbi movement in Indonesia, waria and gays in Holland (like Filipino bakla in the United States) do not generally participate or even identify with modern global gay activist networks constructed around a human rights agenda.

LESBI

The emergence of various "gay" and *lesbi* identities in Indonesia is a complex process, dating back perhaps 30 years (Boellstorff 2003). Lesbi is an Indonesian rendering of lesbian, sometimes defined as "women who love women" but is more generally used to describe female-bodied individuals who identify as men, or masculine females; their female partners may also be called lesbi, or remain unmarked. The representation of these identities in the Indonesian mass media and on the Internet has resulted in the increasing visibility of male and female homosexual and transgendered identities. Lesbi (and gay) identities in Indonesia initially had little or no connection to local or international political activism, though this is changing for both males (Boellstorff 2005a:92) and females (Wieringa 2008). While gay males do occupy some public spaces, such as parks or bus stations, lesbis are mostly invisible, consistent with the Indonesian gender norm that women should not assert themselves in public but remain in the domestic sphere (Davies 2007:48–60).

Much recent ethnography on sex/gender diversity in Indonesia not only focuses on nonnormative gender roles as cultural categories but also emphasizes the personally experienced identities of such roles (Boellstorff 2005a; Peletz 2009; Blackwood 1998; Noor 2012), particularly among lesbi women. With the Indonesian cultural emphasis on normative gender roles for men and women, rather than on heterosexuality per se, same-sex desire is largely overlooked, as it has been historically, as long as it does not threaten "family values" and, for women particularly, is not enacted in public (Penrose 2001). Indonesian women who play the feminine role in lesbi relationships (similar to most gay men) generally marry heterosexually. Indeed, many do not see their homosexual desire as incompatible with such marriages (Boellstorff 2005a:32; Blackwood 2005).

The normative gender binary is essential in shaping the roles and identities of Indonesian lesbis. The masculine partners in such relationships are variously called **tombois** ("tomboys"; like the toms of Thailand), or *hunters*; "tomboy" emphasizes their generally masculine behavior while "hunter" emphasizes their aggressive masculinity in seeking out feminine partners. Similar to waria, tombois report having rejected feminine interests since childhood. In addition to adopting masculine dress, tombois engage in masculine activities; they hang out with young men, smoking, drinking, playing cards, and they go out alone at night, a male prerogative. They may pride themselves on being brave, like men, for example, in resisting family and public pressure to marry; many consider themselves as men who attract "the opposite sex," that is, feminine women.

A study of approximately 100 lower-class lesbis in Jakarta in the 1980s, and later in the late 1990s, reaffirms the importance of normative gender roles in Indonesian lesbi relationships—that of a masculine and a feminine partner (similar to the Western butch/femme relationships in the 1980s), which is basic to the cultural construction of the Indonesian family (Wieringa 2008). The masculine partner adopts men's clothing, hair cut, and body language, and many wrap their breasts so as to seem flat chested. They take on the normative male role of financial responsibility and also claim the male prerogative to engage in sex outside their "marital" relationships.

Their femme partners adopt a woman's role in the extreme: They dress in an exaggeratedly feminine fashion, in frilly and fancy dresses; wear heavy makeup and high heels; and work in feminine fields like selling cosmetics or as secretaries. They also actively participate in women's activities such as voluntary neighborhood associations. Because femmes are attracted by the masculinity of their partners, they easily identify as women and cite sexual satisfaction with their masculine partners as an important reason for maintaining these relationships.

Almost all the masculine lesbis interviewed by anthropologist Saskia Wieringa described themselves as having the "soul of a man," but they also attribute their masculine identities and interest in women to a same-sex erotic attraction. Furthermore, romantic love, or "feelings," is also important in these relationships, a pattern prominent in the mass media and also part of the widely, if vaguely, known Javanese court culture that contains mythic stories of heterosexual love.

Unlike gay men, there are no public spaces available to lesbis; most of the lesbi couples in Jakarta choose the path of "silence" rather than "coming out." This silence is partly motivated by the desire of many lesbi couples to be "assimilated," but it is also a practical response to the increasing hostility of Islam against nonnormative gender roles and identities. Perhaps more important, as in Thailand, maintaining "silence" about lesbi relationships is consistent with the Indonesian value on acting in ways that do not cause open conflict. This silence is slowly changing, however, partly, as in Malaysia, under the pressure of a modern, globalized feminist movement (Wieringa 2008:83; Peletz 2009).

Anthropologist Evelyn Blackwood describes lesbi couples among the Minangkabau, a matrilineal ethnic group in West Sumatra. Blackwood's ethnography generally confirms the importance of the normative Indonesian gender binary in lesbi relationships, modified somewhat in this rural setting (Blackwood 1998, 2010). Here, the tombois identify as men, look and dress like men, and act with the freedom of mobility associated with men. Tombois distinguish themselves from men only by their physical differences; most tombois said they were drawn to their girlfriends by their femininity. Tombois move in public spaces that are associated with men and exclude women, such as pool halls. They typically work in male occupations—as wage laborers, drivers, and parking attendants—although also in occupations acceptable for females, such as cooks and petty traders. Tombois support themselves financially and also give financial help to their families and their girlfriends.

The girlfriends of tombois regard themselves as normal women; they dress in casual feminine style and have the quiet and modest demeanor of the ideal Indonesian woman, a contrast with feminine les-bis in Jakarta, perhaps more suited to a rural style. They, like the Jakarta feminine partners in lesbi relationships, are committed to and enact the Indonesian—and Islamic—gender binary and are drawn to their partners because of their masculinity. Consistent with the femi-nine gender role, the girlfriends of tombois do not "hang out" with friends in public and are almost always accompanied by a female rela-tive or close female friend when they go out. These women prefer female activities such as cooking or handicrafts, although they may become petty traders as well, providing income for themselves and their families.

Among the matrilineal Minangkabau, women's roles in the kin-ship system are so important that a woman's gender transgression is completely rejected as legitimate and does not excuse her from the dom-inant cultural requirement of marriage and reproduction. One's biolog-ical sex as a female defines one's gender: A "real woman" has female genitalia, desires men, marries, bears children, and acts like a woman.

The strict construction of the masculine and the feminine was embodied in the construction of the family under Dutch colonialism and is central to contemporary conservative versions of Islam. Since the 1960s, this emphasis has also incorporated medicalized discourses on AIDS prevention, which strongly encourages premarital chastity and monogamy and increases hostility to all forms of sex/gender diver-sity in Indonesia. Only very recently, and to some extent in alliance with political feminism, have lesbis in Indonesia (as in Malaysia) iden-tified themselves with an international activist discourse based on human rights. This ideology was almost previously unknown and unimagined in Indonesia (Peletz 2009).

As much recent ethnography suggests, the future of alternative sex/gender roles in Indonesia, including bissu, waria, and gay/lesbi relationships, is uncertain. In the past ten years there has been unprec-edented violence against gay Indonesians (Boellstorff 2004b; Davies 2010), emphasizing a new, "masculinist" ideology of national belonging. How these new, Western-generated forms of gender diversity will fare in the future depends partly on how struggles for democracy and justice unfold and the ways in which Indonesia is impacted by political Islam and involvement in the global economy.

Review and Reflection

1. Describe the main similarities and differences between bissu, waria, gay, and lesbi in Indonesia in terms of social roles, identifying behavior, recruitment to the role, and personal identity.

2. Explain the effects of Hinduism, Christianity, and Islam on views of sex/gender diversity in Indonesia. (Looking back: Compare the relationship

of Islam to hijras in Bangladesh with that of waria in Indonesia.) In your judgment have these foreign elements had negative, positive or mixed effects on Indonesian gender diversity; support your view with specific examples.

3. Outline Indonesian historical chronology, indicating how each historical period and political leader affected ideas and attitudes toward gender diversity.

4. Discuss the effects of globalization, for example, the media, the Internet, European colonialism, and the contemporary diaspora, on Indonesian waria.

5. Looking back: Describe the importance of the family and kinship in Polynesia, Indonesia, and the Philippines. How do these cultural ties affect the behavior of gender diverse individuals in these societies? Compare this with the relationship of hijras to Indian/Bangladesh patterns of family and kinship.

6. Looking back and looking forward: Compare the notion of "performing gender identity" as it refers to sex/gender diversity in India, Thailand, the Philippines, Tonga, and Indonesia. Can you describe any examples of "performing gender identity" as it exists in Euro-American culture?

Chapter Seven

Sex/Gender Diversity in Euro-American Cultures

The Euro-American view that there are only two sexes and two genders and that the distinctions between male and female, man and woman, are natural, unchangeable, universal, and desirable is reflected in popular culture and, until the mid-twentieth century, dominated the biological and social sciences (Herdt 1996a). The dominance of this dichotomy largely erased the historical knowledge of alternative sex/gender ideologies.

It has been persuasively argued that a one-sex model, that of "a male/masculine body and mind inscribed on the incomplete and subordinate female body," has roots in European antiquity and persisted up until the Middle Ages (Laqueur 1990). In ancient Greece one- and two-gender models existed side by side. Aristotle, for example, although rooted in the Greek gender ideology of binary opposites, nevertheless conceptualized a one-gender model in his view of sexuality as an ascending ladder of perfection. Women and girls were at the bottom of the ladder; further up were boys and adolescent males; aristocratic men were at the top (Bullough and Bullough 1993:46). The one-sex model is also implied in the Genesis story, in which Adam creates Eve from his own loins. In Plato's *Symposium*, however, Aristophanes argues that three sexes were part of an original human nature: "man, woman, and the union of the two . . . having a double nature" (Buchanan 1977:143).

Other models of sex/gender diversity emerged in different historical periods. In the sixteenth and seventeenth centuries, northern European culture identified three sexes—male, female, and hermaphrodite—and two genders—man and woman (Trumbach 1996). All three biological sexes were assumed capable of having sexual relations with males and females, though each was ordinarily presumed to have sexual relations only with the opposite gender. It was believed that those born biologically intersexed could change their gender, but if hermaphrodites continually switched their gender and took sexual partners of both genders, they were treated as having committed the crime of sodomy. The interests of the state and the Church in upholding the dominant hierarchical and patriarchal sex/gender system was a key factor in European attitudes toward sex/gender diversity, hence the prosecution of intersexed gender switchers.

By the late-seventeenth century, concepts of gender diversity centered on the relationship between male same-sex sexual practices and cross-gender behavior. Up until the early 1700s adult men who engaged in sexual relations with both men and women suffered no loss in their masculine gender status because the predominant form of these relationships, in which adult men sexually penetrated younger boys, did not violate the hierarchical, patriarchal gender code that governed relations between men and women (Trumbach 1998). But adult men who allowed themselves to be penetrated (a subordinate position associated with women) and who exhibited some feminine behaviors were classified in the stigmatized gender variant category of hermaphrodite. In this premodern period, male hermaphroditism was viewed as a quality of the mind and did not refer, as it does today, to biological or anatomical qualities.

Historically, in Euro-American cultures, male homosexuality was associated with effeminacy and gender variance. This group of gay police officers in the New York City gay pride parade demonstrates how this concept has changed. (Photograph by Serena Nanda.)

The term "hermaphrodite" as applied to women also signified gender infractions such as wearing masculine-looking clothing but did not necessarily imply homosexual desire as it did for men. But women who desired women, especially if they dressed or acted like men, were believed to be anatomical hermaphrodites (in contrast to the psychological hermaphroditism of males) and were often medically examined for evidence of masculine biology, such as an enlarged clitoris (Trumbach 1996).

Sex/gender diversity was thus associated with sexual object choice and cross-gender behavior. Although at this time male gender variants were called hermaphrodites and not homosexuals, the association between same-sex sexual desire and effeminacy continued in various forms well into the twentieth century.

By around 1700, when the acceptance of age-structured homosexual relations among males declined, this desire became associated with the social role of the *molly*, which was considered an illegitimate third gender category. The molly was an effeminate man whose sexual preference as an adult was to take the passive sexual role with adult male partners; somewhat later, the role of the *sapphist*—a woman who preferred female sexual partners—emerged. The two "illegitimate" genders of the molly (or sodomite) and the sapphist were added to the two legitimate genders of man and woman, resulting in a system of four genders and two sexes (male and female). By 1800, gender was firmly defined by sexuality: Masculine and feminine gender roles included sexual desire for the opposite gender, while sodomites and sapphists were defined by their sexual preferences for members of their own sex, in conjunction with other cross-gender behaviors. Male desire for another male and the associated effeminacy was viewed as a result of the "corruption" of an individual's mind that had occurred in his early experience, not as a result of any anatomical or biological deficiencies (Trumbach 1996).

By the mid-nineteenth century, Darwinian evolution and Victorian culture combined to shape a European sex/gender ideology that emphasized the opposition of two sexes—male and female—and two genders—man and woman—as functional for the reproduction and survival of the species. The Darwinian emphasis on complementary roles in reproduction rigidified the differences between male and female as innate and far ranging and cemented the definition of "normal" sexuality as the attraction of opposites. Within this framework some sexual reformers and scientific sexologists constructed homosexuality as a third, intermediate gender role in attempt to "naturalize" it and thus undermine public hostility (Hekma 1996). Homosexuality was seen as "a kind of interior androgyny, a hermaphroditism of the soul" (Foucault, quoted in Herdt 1996a:77), an inversion consisting of "a female soul enclosed in a male body."

The association of homosexuality with gender inversion was widely accepted by the emerging profession of psychiatry, though at the time it was rejected by many homosexuals who argued that homosexual practice was associated not only with masculinity but even with a heightened virility. Nevertheless, the theory of homosexuality as sexual inversion remained firmly in place until the mid-twentieth century and, as noted for Thailand, for example, later spread to non-Western societies. The construction of homosexuals as a third gender did not, however, accomplish the aims of its advocates. Under the influence of Darwinian dimorphism—the Victorian identification of masculinity with desire for the opposite sex and the psychiatric characterization of inversion as pathology (see Bullough and Bullough1993:213ff)—the categorization of homosexuals as a third, intermediate category did little to help their public image. Indeed, the association of homosexuality with effeminacy impeded popular acceptance of homosexuals who were now doubly stigmatized: by the shame of their "abnormal" sexual leanings and by their lowered status as women (Hekma 1996). Only after the 1960s did homosexual practices break loose from their associations with cross-gender behavior and cross-gender identity, applied to both males and females.

Although European culture focused on male gender variants, female gender variants appear throughout European (and American) history. While some female gender variant roles, such as the sapphist of eighteenth-century London, were at least partly defined by their sexual attraction to other women, other European female gender variants, like the transvestite female saints of the Middle Ages and the "sworn virgin" of the Balkans (and the Indian sādhin) were defined by their renunciation of sexuality.

TRANSVESTITE FEMALE SAINTS

Beginning in the early-1700s in Europe many cases came to light of women who dressed and passed as men in order to engage in male occupations, particularly as soldiers and sailors, from which they were otherwise barred. Such women were generally stigmatized for subverting the normal gender order and if found out in their "deceits" (which frequently involved marrying a woman under false pretenses) were tried and punished in court.

But in the Middle Ages, the role of a transvestite female had gained cultural approval. Despite the biblical injunction in Deuteronomy against wearing clothes of the opposite sex, transvestite female saints were a significant historical fact and the stuff of legend, fulfilling the words of St. Jerome that "a woman who wishes to serve Christ more than the world . . . will cease to be a woman and will be called a man" (Garber 1992:214; Gregg 1997:151). Pelagia was a female transvestite saint said to have been a prostitute who changed her ways, converted to Christianity, changed her name to (the male) Pelagius, and dressed as a man, wearing a hair shirt beneath her male clothing. Only her death revealed her to be a woman (Bullough and Bullough 1993:52).

St. Eugenia, like other female transvestite saints, cross-dressed in order to join an all-male religious community. She later became an abbot, and only when she was accused of rape by a rich lady who desired her, did she reveal herself as a woman. Theodora, wife of a rich Alexandrite, was another transvestite holy woman. Falsely accused of adultery by a young man whose sexual advances she rejected, Theodora shaved her head, dressed in male clothing, and entered a monastery as a monk. Here she was again falsely accused, this time by a maidservant whose sexual advances she rejected. Theodora was expelled from the abbey, but upon her death her true sex was revealed by angels and she was reinstated as a subject of religious devotion (Gregg 1997:149–50).

Some female transvestite saints were said to have beards (Garber 1992:214); among the most prominent was St. Wilgefortis, who wished to remain a virgin and devote herself to a contemplative life but whose father insisted on her marrying the King of Sicily. Wilgefortis's prayer for deliverance was answered by the sudden growth of a long moustache and beard. When the Sicilian King noticed this, in spite of her veiling, he rejected her, and her father had her crucified. In England St. Wilgefortis is the patron saint of married women who wish to be rid of their husbands.

While psychoanalytical interpretations of these stories, particularly as they involve false accusations of sexuality, have to do with the fantasies of the clerics who told them (see Anson 1974), they exhibit a common feature of patriarchal society, which sanctioned cross-dressing for women, who thereby gained higher status, but not for men, who thereby lost status (Bullough and Bullough 1993:52); there were no cross-dressed male saints (Garber 1992). A common pattern in the lives of transvestite female saints was their gender crossing during a moment of personal crisis, marking a break with a former existence. This pattern fits the most famous cross-dressed saint, Joan of Arc, who like her transvestite models of the Christian monastic tradition broke with her parents, refused to marry the husband they had chosen for her, and "rejected male domination even as she assumed male privilege" (Garber 1992:215). Although sharing many features with other transvestite saints, St. Joan did not try to pass as a man but rather insisted that she was a woman in men's clothes. Her transvestism, which was the source of her "subversive" strength, was considered an abomination by the Church and she was put on trial. "[St. Joan] was usurping a man's function but shaking off the trammels of his sex altogether to occupy a different, third order, neither male nor female, like the angels" (Garber 1992:216).

THE SWORN VIRGIN OF THE BALKANS

Similar in some ways to the gender crossing of transvestite saints were the *sworn virgins* of the Balkans. Biological females, wearing men's clothing and sometimes carrying men's weapons, engaging in men's occupations, and being recognized as men, have been reported in the western Balkans since the early-nineteenth century and function in such roles today (Gremaux 1996; Zhang 2012; Peters 2013). Basically a peasant farming and pastoral region, the western Balkans had a harsh warrior culture involving continuous blood feuds and intergroup killing. Women had few rights, and because society was organized into corporate localized patrilineages, women remained social outsiders throughout their lives. Because women were unarmed, however, they were considered inviolable from assault.

Within this context (and in some places perhaps related to a shortage of males), an institutionalized form of gender crossing emerged in which female sworn virgins assumed a male social identity with the tacit approval of their families and the larger community. The sworn virgin or "manlike woman" vowed to abstain from matrimony and motherhood and to lead a virginal life. She was sometimes called "she who stays," referring to her choice to remain in her natal home and become the heir for a family that had no sons (in contrast to the normal Balkan patrilocal system where a wife lives with her husband's patrilineage). Violation of chastity by a sworn virgin could bring death by stoning.

Rene Gremaux (1996) describes one such female gender crosser: Tonë, a sworn virgin who lived into the mid-twentieth century and whose life exhibited some of the common patterns of this role. Tonë was the first child of a couple who later had two sons, both of whom died in childhood. Because she had no brothers, at age nine Tonë decided to become her parents' son, with her parents' approval. She promised never to marry and began to wear boys' clothing; she retained her female name, though she/he was referred to with the male pronoun. Instead of women's tasks, Tonë helped his father with male tasks and received weapons from his father at the age of 15. Over the years Tonë's voice, posture, and manner of speaking changed so that it was hard to distinguish him from a biological male.

Tonë played the full gamut of male roles and was recognized and honored as a man in his community. He took care of and protected his younger sisters and a younger brother born to his parents late in life. When his sisters married, Tonë, as the older brother, handed each over to her groom. During World War II, Tonë commanded an all-male fighter unit resisting Communist control. He was subsequently captured and much to his dismay was treated as a woman for the year he remained in prison. Upon his release he set up a communal household (away from his area of birth) with his younger brother and acted as "master of the house," receiving guests and participating in traditional all-male gatherings. Outdoors he performed only male tasks, like the heavy and prestigious work of mowing and stacking hay. Although he cooked, he did not engage in women's handicrafts. He also sang "mountaineer songs" and played the lute, traditionally male activities that became a specialty of many Albanian sworn virgins. Tonë was buried with the blessings of the Catholic Church as a virgin and in a male costume as he requested, although he was denied the last honors of a man: The rules of the tribe in the area in which he lived did not allow a biological female to be lamented with the traditional funeral oration by males.

Gremaux (1996:268) explains the sworn virgin role as growing out of a strongly male-dominated culture in which the disappearance of the "house" without any sons was a distressing and stigmatizing event. In these patriarchal cultures (as in the medieval Church), virginity was

Jill Peters visited the mountain villages of northern Albania where she photographed *burneshas* or females who live their lives as men and who take a lifelong vow of celibacy. (Photograph by Jill Peters.)

synonymous with the male virtues of purity and strength. The sworn virgin role, like the Indian sādhin, prevented children from being born out of wedlock and thus from having no legitimate place within a patrilineal social organization in which children were believed to "spring from the blood of the father." While the sexuality of many sworn virgins was not known, the fear of pregnancy very likely restrained their heterosexual relationships, and it is possible that some were sexually attracted to other women.

In the Balkans (as in India), where women are expected to marry and become dependent on men, female adult virginity is a gender anomaly—a "problem" that can be "solved" by constructing virgin adult women as social males. Clearly, though, the main function of this institutionalized third gender role was to enable the maintenance of a patrilineal and patrilocal society by channeling female gender nonconformity and by providing the availability of an heir where there was no son. Sworn virgins inherited real estate (denied to married women, widows, and divorcees) and were expected to safeguard the family property, handing it down to appropriate male heirs. Although most sworn virgins reacted defensively to any reference to their femaleness, in some ways their female sex/gender status was acknowledged: Although sworn virgins were permitted to carry arms, a man who killed or injured one intentionally was looked down on. Rather than merely a gender crosser, the sworn virgin of the Balkans appears to be an example of that culturally "creative bricolage" that is the essential criteria of sex/gender diversity.

TRANSSEXUALISM

Cultures vary in their response to the "problem" of people with sex/gender anomalies—individuals who do not fit into the sex/gender binary or who wish to be of a sex and gender category different from that which is consistent with their anatomy. In Euro-American culture, the solution to this dilemma was the invention of the *transsexual*, which is defined as "the conviction of a biologically normal person of being a member of the opposite sex" (Robert Stoller, quoted in Kessler and McKenna 1978:115), a definition that admits no possibility of an in-between sex or gender. While the term is used in popular and scholarly media to refer to a person who is in a transitional status, moving from one sex to the other, the reconstructive genital surgery that transsexuals desire aims at moving them from just such a transitional state to the status of a "real" man or woman, a gender reversal ultimately confirmed by surgically constructed sex organs and secondary sexual characteristics of the opposite sex.

The term "gender identity," which refers to the inner psychological conviction of an individual that he or she is now transformed into a person of the "opposite sex," is useful in expressing the way in which transsexuals see themselves. Drawing on the mind/body split central in Western culture, gender identity, up until the mid-twentieth century, was associated with the mind—or the soul—as distinguished from the body. With the emergence of transsexual surgery, this concept was useful in confirming the association between the physical transformation and the psychological transformation for a skeptical public and permitted Western society to sustain the view (some would say illusion) that gender, like sex, is dichotomous and permanent, even if sex can be changed (Shapiro 1991). The concept of gender identity permitted the conflict experienced by transsexuals to be understood as a discordance between anatomy and subjectively experienced gender: Transsexuals view the male or female organs as "merely" a mistake that must be corrected in order to align their anatomy with their gender identity.

Psychological professionals were central in defining a transsexual as a woman (or man) trapped in the body of a man (or woman) (Bolin 1988), a definition, diffused in the popular culture and confirmed in transsexual autobiographies. But the notion of the transsexual as a person who has *always* experienced him- or herself in terms of the "opposite" is not entirely supported by the ethnographic data, which indicates that transsexuals do not begin the process of sex transformation with fully formed identities of the opposite gender (Bolin 1996a:449). Rather (like hijras [Nanda 1996]), transsexuals gradually acquire transformed identities as they become involved in transsexual groups and go through the various steps that are part of the process of a sex change.

Anthropologist Anne Bolin (1988) identifies this transformation as a rite of passage in which an individual moves from one social status to another. For the male transsexual, there is a gradual movement from a partial and perhaps ambivalent feminine identity to an identity as a transsexual and, finally, to an identity as a complete woman. These gender identity changes are accompanied by gender role changes: The individual moves from outwardly occupying a male role while secretly dressing as a woman; to more frequently dressing as a woman, perhaps passing as a woman in public; to occupying the roles of both man and woman, while increasingly passing as a woman; to the final social identity transformation into full-time status as a woman. At each stage, a parallel gradual transformation takes place as the biological male is feminized by hormones and finally with sex-change surgery and surgical construction of a vagina, achieving the physical, psychological, and behavioral dimensions of full womanhood (Bolin 1996a:450).

In the United States from the 1960s through the 1980s, this process was monitored by psychological and medical professionals at prestigious, university-affiliated gender clinics that were connected with hospitals where most transsexual surgery was performed; these professionals became the "gatekeepers" of American sex/gender crossing. In most of these clinics, which offered services only for male-to-female transsexuals, when the professionals decided that transsexual surgery was the proper therapy for individuals who presented gender identity problems, they treated preoperative transsexuals with hormones and psychological counseling for two years before permitting them to undergo sex-change surgery (Shapiro 1991). Individuals who expressed ambivalence or confusion about their gender identity might be disqualified for surgery.

Male transsexuals needed to convince the mental health professionals that they had experienced themselves as women from childhood, as far back as they could remember. They also had to demonstrate that they could live full time and be accepted socially as women. This evidence supported a clinical evaluation that an individual was indeed a transsexual (and not "merely" a heterosexual transvestite or a homosexual female impersonator, conditions for which transsexual surgery was considered counterproductive). Because most medical and mental health specialists were committed to a conventional view of the Western sex/gender dichotomy their monitoring process contributed to the stereotypically defined femininity that research indicates most transsexuals exhibit.

In clinical practice and within the male transsexual community, transsexuals viewed themselves as authentic women, in opposition to gay female impersonators, for example, whom they saw as only "playing at" being women. Transsexuals also distinguished themselves from heterosexual cross-dressers (clinically designated transvestites) who did not have a "real" feminine identity and only cross-dressed for purposes of erotic satisfaction. For male transsexuals, the desire for bodily change became the hallmark of authentic feminine gender identity, a desire that rested on, and furthered, the Euro-American association of gender with biological sex. Transsexuals, then, far from being an example of gender diversity, both reflected and reinforced the dominant Euro-American sex/gender ideology in which one had to choose to be either a man or a (stereotypical) woman.

Transsexualism has been largely a male phenomenon, partly because female-to-male sex reassignment surgery developed much later than male-to-female sex reassignment surgery and is generally less aesthetically and surgically effective (Lothstein 1983:6–7). But this in itself may be an artifact of a male-dominated culture in which male gender dysfunction creates more anxiety than female gender dysfunction and is a problem society is more willing to solve (Garber 1992:103). The emphasis on male transsexualism also results from the different social pressures on gender conformity: It is easier for female (preoperative) transsexuals as masculine women than it is for male preoperative transsexuals with a female gender identity to adapt to a male-oriented society. Furthermore, because it is—or was, certainly until the mid-twentieth century—considered natural by the psychiatric profession in patriarchal Euro-American societies for women to wish to become men, women's desires for sex transformations did not seem as indicative of a severe *psychological* disorder and therefore were not as clinically urgent as men's (Lothstein 1983:6–7).

The availability of the sex-change operation and the emergence of the "transsexual" helps sustain the dominant Euro-American sex/gender system based on binary opposites (Kessler and McKenna 1978). The new male or female sex status may be supported by the construction of a revised life story and certain legal changes, such as revising one's sex on the birth certificate, though this has been repudiated by some American courts. In 2002, for example, a Kansas state court rejected the claim of a transsexual to inherit her husband's property on the basis that her transsexual status did not meet the Kansas legal requirement that only recognizes marriage between persons of the opposite sex. The court acknowledged that, "While [the defendant though] born male, wants and believes herself to be a woman . . . her female anatomy is all man made . . . and thus as a matter of law, [the defendant] is a male" (quoted in Norgren and Nanda 2006:200).

Transsexualism reflected and reinforced the Euro-American cultural view that genitals were the defining feature of gender: In Western culture, gender attribution is genital attribution (Kessler and McKenna 1978). In spite of the many other "invisible" determinants of biological sex now known (chromosomes, hormones), it is the genitals as the *visible* indicators of sex that make them so important in gender identity and presentation, hence the emphasis on surgery by both medical and mental-health professionals as well as by transsexuals themselves, an emphasis that reproduces the "biological imperative of Euro-American sex/gender ideology" (Bolin 1996a:454, 455).

TRANSGENDERISM

The dominance of transsexualism as a sex/gender alternative role is now sharing the stage with ***transgenderism***, a concept now widespread and well established in contemporary Euro-American popular culture and academe. Transgenderism is both an individual and a collective phenomenon—individuals experience alternative sex/gender identities and individual transgendered voices have become part of a new, exploding, activist movement with implications in law, sports, employment discrimination, health care, social class, and many other features of American life (Williams 2011; Murray 2011; Currah and

Gender mixing, whether seriously or in play, provokes
reflection on the culturally constructed nature of sex and gender roles. (Photograph by
Serena Nanda.)

Stryker 2014). Transgenderism has its foundation in the ancient tradition of androgyny, a view that has made the crosscultural data from
anthropology—with its descriptions of the positive value of androgyny
in some other cultures—particularly relevant to the transgender community (Bolin 1996b:39; Connor 1993; Feinberg 1996).

Unlike transsexuals, *transgenderists* (*transpeople*) do not consider themselves limited to a choice of one of two genders. Transgenderism includes a wide continuum of options, from individuals who wish to
undergo sex reassignment surgery to those who wish to live their lives
androgynously. Anthropologist Daniel Valentine (2007) begins his ethnography on transgenderism by noting that every person in the first
transgender group he engaged with defined themselves differently from
all the others. The previous split between transsexuals and "part-time"
gender crossers who did not wish sex reassignment surgery has been
mooted to some extent by transgenderism, which validates a range of
gender roles and identities within society and even within an individual.

Transgenderists can be narrowly defined as persons who want to
change gender roles without undergoing sexual reassignment surgery;
they can also be defined as "persons who steer a middle course, living
with the physical, social, and psychological traits of both genders. Most
transpeople differentiate themselves from "gay" or "transvestites," but
Valentine found examples of individuals who did so identify them-

selves, within the wider transgender community. Thus, transgenderism is an inclusive term describing those "who may alter their anatomy with hormones or surgery" but also those who intentionally retain many of the characteristics of the gender to which they were originally assigned. Many transpeople lead part-time lives in both genders; most cultivate an androgynous appearance (Bolin 1996a:466).

Transgender identities vary widely, but the philosophy of transgenderism is well summarized in the words of one transperson who says: "You no longer have to fit into a box . . . it is okay to be transgendered. You can now lay anywhere on the spectrum from non-gendered to full transsexual" (Bolin 1996a:475). Transgenderists view gender and sex categories, or "boxes," as improperly imposed by society and its "sexual identity gatekeepers" referred to above. Unlike transsexuals of the 1970s and 1980s, transgenderists today challenge and stretch the boundaries of the American binary system of sex/gender oppositions and renounce the American definition of gender as dependent on a consistency of genitals, body type, identity, role behaviors, and sexual orientation. Indeed, transgenderists reject any societal attempt to circumscribe an individual's identity and capabilities by what a culture deems to be masculine or feminine behavior (Feinberg 1996). While in one sense transpeople are increasingly acknowledged in American society, there is also harassment and even violence against them.

INTERSEXUALITY

Congruent with transgenderism is a revisiting of biological *intersexuality*, which was previously defined as the condition of having ambiguous genitalia (Dreger 1998; Kessler 1998; Fausto-Sterling 2000). Today, the definition includes those born with a combination of what are typically considered male and female sex traits, the most visible being the genitals but also including gonadal or chromosomal traits (Karkazis 2008; Reis 2009). Twentieth-century developments in genital surgery, gonadal surgery, and hormonal interventions provided clinicians with the tools to "fix" individuals identified as intersexed at birth or in very early childhood, which was consistent with the dominant medical and psychological opinion that holds that gender identity is learned early, that it is permanent once learned, and that a gender identity consistent with one's anatomy is a basic condition for adult mental health (see Money and Ehrhardt 1972). As a result of these assumptions, medical practice was almost completely committed to the view that sex assignment should be as early as possible, in infancy or early childhood, and that surgical intervention is recommended to shape the intersexed infant into a boy or a girl.

An intensely moving ethnography by anthropologist Katrina Karkazis (2008), based on interviews both in the medical profession and among intersexed individuals and their parents, raises important questions about the negative impact this medical perspective imposed on intersexed individuals. Acknowledging that medical interventions were often well intentioned, Karkazis shows that they were rooted in the conventional American sex/gender binary and did not account for other possibilities. Indeed, she convincingly demonstrates that both sex and gender are culturally constructed and that "fixing sex" is not the only, or even the most appropriate, response to intersexed individuals.

The value of medical alterations in anatomy is now a subject of debate in the popular culture, in the scientific community (Dreger 1998), and among governments. In 1997, for example, members of the Intersex Society of North America lobbied Congress to extend a recent federal ban on genital cutting, aimed mainly at African cultural practices of clitoridectomy, to American pediatric surgeons who customarily reduce or remove infant clitorises deemed "abnormally" large, a practice affecting about 2,000 babies a year (Angier 1997:C1). The issues in the debate are about who has the right to decide what are aesthetically acceptable genitalia, whose interests are served by surgical intervention, and whether sex/gender identity is so intertwined with the appearance of the genitals that it is worth subjecting infants or children to this operation. Some persons who have experienced this surgery maintain that the negative effects (for example, a lack of clitoral sensation) are not worth the aesthetic results. As with transsexualism, medical clinicians become gatekeepers of the Euro-American sex/gender dichotomy, in this case by surgically "normalizing" anomalous individuals at birth (Kessler 1998).

Partly in response to these types of debates, several governments have altered their laws regarding the listing of gender on official documents. In Australia and New Zealand, for example, individuals have the option of selecting "X" as their gender on their passports; in Bangladesh, there is a gender option for passports called "other"; Nepal has a third-gender option on its census forms; Pakistan has a third-gender option on its national identification cards; and India added a third-gender category to its voting lists. Most recently, Germany created an "indeterminate sex" category by permitting parents to leave the gender category blank on birth certificates, the first European country to do so.

The ways that transsexuality and intersexuality are managed by the medical, psychological, and legal professions illuminates Euro-American beliefs regarding gender and genitals (Greenberg 2012). Yet, these beliefs, like those in any culture, are subject to change, as we have seen with the emergence of transgenderism, the impact of intersex activists, and the small but growing changes in national laws, as indicated above (BBC News Europe 2013).

One important factor in change is the now well-publicized diversity of alternative sex/gender identities and the various combinations of gender identity and sexual orientations documented within male-to-female transsexual and transvestite populations in the United States. This diversity, which was masked by the institutional requirements of the sex-change profession, contradicts the rigid differentiations psychological professionals made between transsexuals, effeminate homosexuals, and heterosexual cross-dressers (Bolin 1996a:461).

The closing of university gender clinics affiliated with hospitals doing sex-reassignment surgery permitted new, more variable social constructions of gender diversity to emerge. Private sites for sex-reassignment surgery are more "client centered" and less subject to professional "gatekeeper" decisions about who is psychologically appropriate for such surgery. In addition, in the milieu of identity politics, which has characterized the American social scene in the last 30 years, the organization of transgenderists, intersexuals, and other gender variants has found fertile ground for expansion.

Although sex-change operations achieved the personal desires of transsexuals to become members of the "opposite" sex, in aim and in result, transsexualism upheld rather than challenged the "two-party" sex/gender system of Euro-American culture. But within the transsexual phenomenon were the seeds of transgenderism. Transsexualism began the destabilization of the necessary connection between gender and anatomy and undermined the cultural assumption that the four elements of a sex/gender system—biology, culture, sexuality, and personal identity—were inextricably linked. From these small seeds of doubt, various forms of transgenderism may emerge as the most potentially "subversive" challenge yet to the cultural pattern of the Western binary sex and gender system.

Review and Reflection

1. Describe three models of Western sex/gender diversity beginning with ancient Greece through the mid-twentieth century.

2. Analyze the circumstances and motivations of female cross-dressing during different periods of Euro-American history, from the middle ages through the twentieth century.

3. Using Tonë as an example, describe the characteristics and lifestyle of the sworn virgin of the Balkans. Explain how this role reinforces the male-dominated culture of the Balkans. (Looking back: Compare this role and its effects on gender ideology with that of the sādhin in India.)

4. Define the differences between transsexual, intersex, and transgender. Describe the roles the medical profession, laws, and political activism have played in addressing issues concerning these different types of sex/gender diversity. Explain how these professional ideologies are affecting

changes in social response to these three different types of sex/gender diversity in the West.

5. Explain and analyze how transsexualism, intersexuality, and transgenderism support or undermine the dominant Euro-American sex/gender ideology.

6. In your judgment, what is the future of transgenderism? Support your answer with specific examples in Euro-American cultures and societies

7. Looking back: Discuss the major differences between the concepts of sex/gender diversity in Euro-American society and those in Native America, India/Bangladesh, Brazil, Polynesia, Thailand, the Philippines, and Indonesia.

Chapter Eight

Variations on a Theme

CRITERIA FOR CONSTRUCTING
SEX/GENDER VARIATION

Different cultures use different criteria for constructing diverse sex/gender roles. Genitals (and now other, more invisible biological traits) are central in Euro-American cultures, though the transgender and intersex activist movements provide different approaches to genital surgical interventions as the "solution" to gender ambiguity. Anatomy is perhaps least important among Native Americans and in Polynesia, where cross-gender occupation mainly defines these roles. Biological hermaphroditism is a central starting point in the *cultural* definition of the hijras, the Navajo nádleeh, and the Indonesian waria in defining their gender status, but other, behavioral factors are more important.

The relation of sexuality to gender is complex and varies crossculturally both in normative and nonnormative sex/gender roles (Brownell and Besnier 2013). Hardly any cultures give the homosexual/heterosexual divide the importance it has in the West. In Brazil, Thailand, the Philippines, Indonesia, and Polynesia the stereotype of effeminate males is that they are receptors for oral and anal sex, and today they are sometimes referred to as transgendered homosexuals; their male sexual partners, however, are considered normal men. Indian hijras, although known *sub rosa* to take the receptor role in sex, are not primarily defined by this, though they do seem to be so defined—and empowered—in Bangladesh. Thus, the crosscultural evidence argues against any single type of relationship between homosexuality (same-sex desire and practice) and gender diversity. However, the widespread, if not universal, association between male homosexual relations and

121

gender diversity cannot be lightly dismissed, though it must be examined within a specific cultural context.

While sexuality and accompanying feminine behavior often defines male gender variants, female gender variants, such as the Indian sādhin, the transvestite saints of the European Middle Ages, and the sworn virgin of the Balkans, are defined by the renunciation of sexuality. Among Native Americans sexuality traditionally appears mostly irrelevant in defining gender diversity. Previously largely ignored, nonnormative female sex/gender roles are becoming more visible in Southeast Asia, generally following "normal" gender role behavior.

VARYING DEGREES OF INSTITUTIONALIZATION

Cultures vary in the extent to which sex/gender diversity is governed by relatively consistent and well-known norms that clearly mark gender variant roles as different from those of man and woman. In Native American cultures, gender variants had traditional roles distinct from those of either men or women, and such roles were frequently acknowledged through public rituals.

Hijras occupy a highly institutionalized sex/gender variant role in India, some features of which are shared with hijras in Bangladesh. Hijras are culturally acknowledged as ritual performers, they participate in a formal ritual initiation into the hijra community, and they adopt feminine behavior. The institutionalization of the hijra role is reinforced by their structured and elaborate local and national social networks. The Indonesian bissu is also an institutionalized role, while the waria appears to have moved historically from a liminal effeminate male role to that of a widely recognized and institutionalized gender alternative. Gender variant roles in contemporary Brazil, Polynesia, Thailand, and the Philippines are less institutionalized than the hijras, the bissu, and the waria, but they are widely recognized as culturally defined alternative gender roles. In urban areas, where gender variants may congregate to work, live, or "hang out," gender variant subcultures may develop through frequent social interaction.

PUBLIC RECOGNITION OF
SEX/GENDER TRANSFORMATIONS

Cultures differ in the degree to which they acknowledge the possibility of complete sex/gender crossing. The Euro-American transsexual exemplifies the most extreme of this recognition: Sex-reassignment surgery aims precisely at the reassignment of an individual from one sex to the other, though, as noted, such transformation is not always legally accepted. The Mohave hwame and alyha seem closest to the Euro-American transsexual in their desire to be recognized as members of the "opposite" sex. Yet, in spite of some strenuous efforts by Mohave gender variants to imitate the physiology of the "other" sex, complete sex/gender transformations were not culturally acknowledged and, to some extent, were ridiculed.

In Brazil, both travestís themselves and the public deny complete sex/gender transformation. Like Indonesian waria, travestís do not wish to get rid of their penises, although they go to great lengths to achieve other aspects of female anatomy through the injection of silicone. Travestís control their presentation of their sex/gender role according to their emotional and financial interests. While in deference to the desires of his boyfriend, a travestí will "background" or hide his penis; he may also use it to satisfy his customers if the price is right. While Brazilians express awe regarding the feminine beauty of successful travestís, they also try to shame other travestís by using masculine forms of address, denying their feminine pretensions.

Like travestís, Filipino bakla do not generally undergo sex-reassignment surgery and, like hijras, acknowledge the impossibility of becoming women because they cannot bear children. Yet, bakla feminine presentations, particularly in beauty contests, aim at perfection. Indeed, many Filipino women agree that bakla, in their appropriation of international images of glamour and style, are more successful than ordinary women. At the same time, however, audience awareness of bakla femininity as a performance is always present. In bakla beauty contests, the possibility of a "gender slip" generates a certain amount of tension for contestants and for the audience.

In a very different context, the sworn virgin of the Balkans is also not viewed as a complete gender transformation. Social recognition of the gender change is observed out of respect for the individual's wishes and to accord a family the honor of having continued its "house," but there are occasions, such as Tonë's funeral or the prohibition on killing even an armed sworn virgin, when the acceptance of the sex/gender transformation breaks down.

The Euro-American phenomenon of the complete sex crossover of the transsexual was made possible by the improvement of the medical technology of sex-reassignment surgery. A question arises: If the technology were available, would the partial gender crossing in other cultures be transformed into transsexualism? Some waria, kathoey, and, increasingly, Filipino bakla do wish to undergo transsexual surgery, now available in Malaya and Thailand, but most do not; such surgery is contrary to the Islamic injunction that an individual must remain as he was made by Allah, although it is increasingly available in Iran (Najmabadi 2008).

In the United States there is a growing transgender movement centered on androgyny and nonpermanent gender transformations, which seems to be supplanting transsexualism; indeed, surgical resolution of issues of both transsexuality and intersexuality has recently come under strong criticism.

EXPLAINING SEX/GENDER DIVERSITY

Several different explanations are proposed to account for sex/ gender diversity in different historical and cultural contexts; one is *gender differentiation*. Gender differentiation refers to the extent to which normative gender roles in a society are well defined, specialized, and hierarchical as opposed to fluid, overlapping, and egalitarian. The ethnographic evidence is inconclusive: Sex/gender diversity is found in cultures with both high and low gender differentiation (Munroe and Munroe 1977; Munroe, Whiting, and Hally 1969). India, for example, has high gender differentiation yet also contains several gender variant roles; in contrast, many Native American cultures that have (relatively) low gender differentiation also have a high degree of sex/gender diversity. Similarly, gender diversity appears not only in Polynesia and Southeast Asia, where gender differentiation is relatively low (with many exceptions), but also in Brazil, where gender differentiation is very high. Whereas Unni Wikan (1977) attributes the emergence of xanith in Oman to substantial normative sex/gender differentiation, Evelyn Blackwood (1984) attributes the high number of female Native American gender variants to relatively low gender differentiation in those cultures.

Sex/gender diversity may also be significantly associated with a particular cultural concept of the person. In India, for example, the concept of dharma allows for behavioral flexibility according to each individual's unique situation and past experiences, and sex/gender diversity is viewed as one among many legitimate life paths. Regarding the xanith, Omani culture holds that the world is imperfect; people are created with dissimilar natures and are likewise imperfect, and the gender nonconformist is tolerated and allowed to pursue his or her life in peace. In Polynesian and Native American cultures also, there is less concern with forcing individuals into a mold in which they do not fit, whether by physical anomaly or personal inclination; that is, sex/gender diversity is considered natural and is not subject to moral or legal sanctions. In Polynesia and Southeast Asia, the cultural focus on how individuals play their social roles means that private behavior that does not impinge on the social order is largely left alone.

Cosmology and religion are also associated with the presence or absence of sex/gender diversity. In the Philippines, in Native American cultures, in Afro-Brazilian (and West African) religions, in Hinduism, and in Hindu-influenced cultures like Indonesia, the possibility, and even the power, of sex/gender transformations and androgyny are congenial to the emergence of sex/gender diversity; androgyny—a combination of masculine and feminine—is a powerful symbol in many cultures, often connected with the origin of human beings. Where androgyny is sacred, as in Hinduism and in island Southeast Asia, conditions for the emergence of sex/gender diversity seem favorable. Religion may also suppress or restrict the formation of sex/gender diversity, as in the cases of Orthodox Judaism, Christianity (both Catholicism and evangelical Protestantism), and contemporary forms of conservative Islam.

MALE AND FEMALE GENDER DIVERSITY

The ethnographic evidence for the preponderance of male, compared to female, sex/gender variant roles has several possible, but not necessarily mutually exclusive, explanations. Psychological explanations focus on the more contingent nature of the development of masculinity. Since both males and females are brought up by women, children have a high degree of identification with female gender roles. The development of a mature masculine identity therefore requires a separation from the female; this is not as compelling a factor in the development of feminine identity.

Social explanations highlight the fact that in patriarchal societies, women gain social status by acting like men, while men lose social status by acting like women. Female-to-male gender transformations thus make "social sense" and present less of a "crisis" for the social order than male-to-female transformations. Furthermore, some of the ethnographic imbalance may be due to the androcentric (male-centered) nature of the social sciences, particularly psychology, but also anthropology. Beginning with the work of Margaret Mead, and increasingly with the rise of feminist anthropology in the 1970s, anthropologists such as Micaela di Leonardo and Alice Schlegal, among others, and psychologist Carol Gilligan documented how male bias in research, which often left out women's narratives, led to the distorted view that culture is created by and for men, while women were portrayed as passive or even rendered invisible (Mascia-Lees 2010:46–59). This omission applies even more so to sex/gender diversity, as suggested in this book.

THE FUNCTIONS, ROLES, AND SIGNIFICANCE
OF SEX/GENDER DIVERSITY

As noted throughout this text, alternative sex/gender roles often have special functions: The in-between nature of Native American gender variants was associated with their role as specialists in healing sexual diseases, and they also served as go-betweens in marriage; Indian and Bangladeshi hijras have special ritual roles at childbirth and marriage; and the bissu and waria of Indonesia have important ritual and organizational functions at weddings. The mixed gender of Brazilian bicha also associates them with the sacred transformations involved in possession trance in Afro-Brazilian religions. While contemporary Polynesian and Filipino sex/gender variants do not have sacred roles in their societies, they do have secular ritual roles: In Polynesia they are role models of what men or virgin girls should not be and represent the spontaneous and the unruly in contrast to the norms of restraint, while the Filipino bakla mediate between local and international cultural systems of beauty and style.

The extent to which sex/gender variant roles, especially those of exaggerated feminine male performances like those of hijras or Western "drag queens," challenge sex/gender binaries is subject to debate. On the one hand, sex/gender variants like the Brazilian travestí, the Philippine bakla, the Euro-American transsexual or "drag queen," and the Indonesian lesbi appear to reinforce the heterogender, patriarchal sex/gender binary ideologies in their respective societies. On the other hand, some gender theorists hold that the cross-gender behavior of sex/gender variants, however seemingly humorous, playful, or marginalized, is always subversive, in that it calls attention to the social *construction* of sex and gender (Butler 1990; Garber 1992; Newton 1979; Bakshi 2004). This certainly seems true of the contemporary transgender identity and role in the United States. Yet, other theorists hold that in some societies, such as the precontact Philippines, Polynesia, Native North America, and in traditional Buddhist or Hindu religious thought, the debate is misguided because sex/gender diversity and sex/gender transformations are considered as "natural" as the sex/gender roles of male and female.

GLOBALIZATION

The multiple and complicated processes of globalization affect sex/gender diversity differently in different cultures. One significant factor in globalization is the growing importance of migration. The migration of Indonesian waria to Holland and the migration of Polynesians and Filipino bakla to the United States and Israel (*Paper Dolls* 2006), for example, offer new opportunities for reconstructing sex/gender roles and identities, though the culture of the countries of origin still play an important though subtle role in the ongoing transformation of sex/gender identities in the new destination. These new roles and identities may then be brought back to their countries of origin through return migration or temporary visits; this in turn has an effect on local cultures. In some cases, the diaspora is created by repressive political conditions in the countries of origin, for example Malaysia (see Peletz 2009:272) or Iran (Shakhsari 2013; Cotton 2012), with the United States the most frequent destination; some American anthropologists have acted as witnesses for those seeking asylum.

The Internet has exploded with new systems of global mass media—e-mail, websites, and blogs—as well as social networking services. Transgender websites offer individuals new ways of thinking about sex/gender diversity. Moreover, social networking websites provide opportunities to create an online profile and meet others with similar interests. In addition to the global giant Facebook, myriad virtual communities exist, many of which are highly popular with transgenderists outside the United States, including Friendster (Indonesia, Philippines, and Thailand), hi5 (Thailand), and Sonico.com (Latin America).

The effects of mass media work both ways: Western media, such as ethnographic film, for example, highlights the exoticness—and acceptability—of diverse sex/gender roles in non-Western cultures. At the same time, Western-based media bring to non-Western societies new ways for nonnormative sex/gender individuals to imagine themselves that go beyond local concepts. The international tourist market also affects local and international concepts of sex/gender diversity, particularly, as illustrated in Thailand, through popular entertainments and sex tourism.

Another important global element affecting change in local concepts of sex/gender diversity is the growing attention given to health concerns, particularly in connection with HIV/AIDS prevention. This effort affects sex/gender diversity in different, sometimes contradictory ways. On the one hand, as in Indonesia and India, the increasing presence of international organizations (e.g., NGOs) and local, government-sponsored health centers accord legitimacy to nonnormative sex/gender individuals and even offer employment to a few (Reddy 2010; Peletz 2009). On the other hand, as in Bangladesh and India, the association of HIV/AIDS with sex/gender diversity emphasizes hijras' deviant sexuality, and the public association of hijras with a dread disease undermines their public acceptance in the wider society (Hossain 2012b:131).

Also receiving increased ethnographic attention is the global emergence of "gay" and "lesbian" identities, sometimes in societies where these roles were formerly unacknowledged, or even unknown. As recent ethnographies make clear, these identities do not necessarily mean everywhere what they do in the West. Among Filipino bakla, for example, the important cultural role of family and kinship persist in migration, and that pattern, as well as others, shapes a strong sense of difference between bakla and American gays.

In many societies, same-sex desire and practice have not been important elements in a definition of sex/gender diversity, and their centrality in nonnormative gender roles is sometimes puzzling or misunderstood by people in more rural or isolated societies, such as Tonga. The increasing visibility of "gay" and "lesbian" roles is also associated with political activism, both gay and feminist, distinctly Western in origin and connected to a human rights agenda, but slowly increasing in non-Western contexts. At the same time, this activist agenda is coming under restrictions in cultures where it is viewed as politically and culturally subversive; Russia is a notable recent example. In documenting emerging as well as traditional forms of sex/gender diversity and in incorporating the interaction of the local and the global, anthropology continues its historical contribution of illuminating the richness, variety, and change in human experiences across cultures.

Review and Reflection

1. Discuss some of the relationships between dominant cultural patterns and the types of sex/gender categories that exist in different societies, using examples from the previous chapters.

2. Explain the most important differences between male and female sex/gender diversity as these exist crossculturally. Why do you think male sex/gender diversity is more frequently found crossculturally than female sex/gender diversity?

3. Analyze the cultural elements that appear to be most importantly related to the institutionalization of sex/gender diversity as a crosscultural phenomenon.

4. Using examples from different chapters, discuss how global patterns, such as HIV/AIDS, feminism, the Internet, migration, tourism, or other patterns, have affected local ideas, practices, and social responses to sex/gender diversity.

5. Compare the relationship of religion and ritual roles to sex/gender diversity in different cultures.

6. Describe some of the ways that contemporary Euro-American concepts of sex/gender diversity seem to be unique and analyze how these may relate to dominant Euro-American cultural patterns.

Glossary

alyha. A male gender variant among the Mohave Indians.

androgyny. The uniting of male and female.

bakla/bantut/bayot. A transgendered male role in the Philippines; the term varies by region.

berdache. A derogatory European term for transgendered Native Americans, now called **two-spirit.**

bicha. See **travestí**.

bissu. An androgynous shaman in Indonesia.

Candomble. An Afro-Brazilian religion in which women and gender variants play important leadership roles.

cross-dresser. An individual who adopts the clothing or accessories commonly associated with the opposite sex/gender in a particular culture for a variety of personal reasons or in a variety of public contexts.

cross-dressing. The act of wearing clothing and accessories commonly associated with the opposite sex/gender as defined within a particular society or culture for a variety of personal motives and/or in a variety of public contexts.

gender. The qualities and roles associated with femininity, masculinity, and alternative roles in a particular society.

gender differentiation. The extent to which gender roles in a society are specialized and hierarchical or fluid and egalitarian.

gender diversity (gender variation). Sex/gender systems that contain more than male and female, masculine and feminine categories.

gendered homosexuality. A sex/gender ideology in which males who take the receptor role in same-sex relations are also expected to, and do, adopt feminine behaviors.

hermaphrodite. A person born with male and female genitalia.

heterosexual. A person whose sexual orientation entails sexual desires toward a person of the opposite sex.

hijra. A male sex/gender variant, neither man nor woman, in India, Pakistan, and Bangladesh.

homosexuality (contemporary Western). A sexual orientation toward a person of the same sex/gender.

hwame. A female gender variant among the Mohave.

intersexuality. A condition in which an individual exhibits biological features, such as genitals and gonads, of both sexes.

kathoey. A Thai gender variant, originally meaning hermaphrodite but now mainly referring to transgendered males.

lesbi. The Indonesian rendering of lesbian, defined as biological females who identify as men or masculine females.

māhū. A primarily male gender variant in Tahiti and Hawai'i.

molly. The illegitimate male gender variant in eighteenth-century England, practicing sodomy and adopting feminine behaviors.

nádleeh. The designation of a variety of sex/gender variants among the Navajo.

passivo. The man who takes the subordinate role in sexual relations in Brazil.

sādhin. A female gender variant associated with virginity in India.

sapphist. An (illegitimate) female gender variant role in eighteenth-century London defined mainly by the adoption of masculine behavior.

sex. The biological aspects of being male, female or other.

sex/gender diversity. Cultural patterns that include roles that transcend male/female and man/and woman binary categories.

sex/gender identity. The relatively consistent, subjective experiencing of oneself as male or female, feminine or masculine, or other.

sexual orientation. A sexual preference for a partner of the same or opposite sex.

sexuality. Can refer to sexual orientation or sexual practices.

sworn virgin. A female-to-male transgendered role in the Balkans.

tomboi. The female bodied, masculine performing partner in a lesbian relationship in Thailand and Indonesia.

transgenderism. A term that includes a wide continuum of options, from individuals who wish to undergo sex reassignment surgery to those who wish to live their lives androgynously.

transgenderists (transpeople). An inclusive sex/gender category in Euro-American societies that includes transsexuals and others who keep both their feminine and masculine characteristics.

transsexual (in Euro-American culture). A person convinced he/she belongs to the gender opposite to that of his/her anatomy (postoperative: a transsexual who undergoes sex-reassignment surgery).

transvestism. Cross-dressing.

transvestite. One who cross-dresses (either sporadically or permanently, and for different psychological or cultural reasons).

travestí. A male transgendered role in Brazil.

two-spirit. A widespread contemporary label for Native American male and female gender variants, previously called berdache.

viado. See **travestí**.

waria. A male bodied person who adopts a feminine persona in Indonesia.

Selected Films

The Adventures of Priscilla, Queen of the Desert. Director, Stephan Elliott. 1994. Gramercy Pictures. Color. 102 minutes. A wonderfully moving and funny film about three "drag queens" on an odyssey across the Australian desert. Available from Movies Unlimited, www.moviesunlimied.com/musite/default.asp?.

Beautiful Boxer. Director, Ekachai Uekrongtham. 2003. Color. 118 minutes. Based on the story of Parinya Charoenphol, who became a champion Muay Thai kickboxer in order to finance his dream of becoming a woman. Released by TLA Entertainment Group, Philadelphia, PA. Available from www.amazon.com.

Bombay Eunuch. Director, Alexandra Shiva. 2001. Color. 71 minutes. In Hindi and Tamil with English subtitles. An interesting, contemporary documentary film on a group of hijras in Bombay, which illuminates the sexual, social, and economic aspect of their lives. Gidalya Pictures, 5 East 9th St., New York, NY 10003.

Eunuchs—India's Third Gender. Director, Michael Yorke. 1991. Under the Sun Series. BBC, London. Color. This highly regarded film focuses on contrasting lifestyles and attitudes of three hijras. It treats the subject generally without sensationalism and reflects the filmmakers' long acquaintance with their subject. Available from: www.bbcactivevideoforlearning.com.

Juggling Gender. Director, Tami Gold. 1992. Color. 30 minutes. Performance artist and bearded woman Jennifer Miller begins this documentary about gender stereotypes in the United States. Distributor: Women Make Movies. Available from Anderson Gold Films, http://andersongoldfilms.com/films/documentaries/jg.htm.

Ke Kulana He Mahu: Remembering a Sense of Place. Producers, Kathryn Xian, Jaymee Carvajal, Brent Anbe, and Connie Florez. 2001. A history of the ways in which colonialism was instrumental in marginalizing the traditional transgender role of the mahu, and how it is being revitalized in contemporary Hawai'i. Available from Zang Pictures, Inc., 4348 Waialae Ave., #248, Honolulu, HA; www.zangpictures.net/projects/kekulanaHeMahu.html.

Ladyboys. Director, Jeremy Marre. 1992. Harcourt Films, London. Color. 51 minutes. A good accompaniment for the chapter on Thailand. The film follows the lives of two young men from a rural area as they join the world of kathoey and a career in the transvestite cabarets in tourist centers of Thailand. Available online in six episodes from BBC Documentaries, www.thedocumentorysite.com/category/bbc.

Ma Vie en Rose (My Life in Pink). Director, Alain Berliner. 1997. Color. 1 hour, 28 minutes. A charming film about a Belgian middle-class family whose seven-year-old

131

son decides that he would like to be a girl. Sony Pictures Entertainment. Available from www.amazon.com.

Mohammed to Maya. Director, Jeff Roy. 2013. This documentary film centers on an Indian Muslim, Mohammed, who undergoes surgery in Thailand to transform him into a woman. Now called Maya, she speaks about her family's negative reactions, her feelings and fears, and her new life as a woman (alert: several scenes of the actual surgery are included). Information about the film is available from http://mohammedtomaya.com.

Paper Dolls. Director, Tomer Heymann. 2006. 80 minutes. A documentary following the lives of five Filipino transgender individuals who emigrated to Israel to work as health care providers for elderly, Orthodox Jewish men and perform as drag queens on their night off. Distributed by Strand Releasing. Available from www.amazon.com.

Paris Is Burning. Director, Jennie Livingston. 1990. Color. 78 minutes. A critically acclaimed film whose subject is the "voguing" subculture of African American and Latino gays in New York City. The film also serves as a poignant commentary on American cultural values. Lionsgate. Available from www.amazon.com.

The Salt Mines. Directors, Susana Aikin and Carlos Aparicio. 1990. Color. 45 minutes. Spanish with subtitles. Through engaging interviews, a picture emerges of the lives of a group of homeless Latino transvestite prostitutes (similar to the travestís of Brazil) who live in the out-of-service sanitation trucks in New York City, which hold the salt for snow removal in the city. Available from frameline, http://cart.frameline.org/ProductDetails.asp?ProductCode=T409.

A Self-Made Man. Director, Lori Petchers. 2013. 56 minutes. At a crucial turning point in his life, Tony Ferriaolo's inner voice said, "Create yourself." This credo once saved his life and now serves as a guiding principle as he educates gender nonconforming youth, as well as their parents. Available from frameline, http://cart.frameline.org/ProductDetails.asp?ProductCode=T918.

Shinjuku Boys. Directors, Kim Longinotto and Jano Williams. 1995. Color. 53 minutes. A compelling documentary film relating the stories of "onnabes," women who live as men and have girlfriends (though they don't usually identify as lesbians) and who work in Shinjuku, Tokyo's pleasure district. Available from Women Make Movies, www.wmm.com/filmcatalog/pages/c222.shmtl.

Taboo: The Third Sex. Writers, Anthony Griffis and Rodney Long. 2009. Episode from a TV Series. National Geographic takes the viewer to India, where hijras marry their god in a festive ritual; then to an Indonesian village that recognizes five genders (included are bissu, as documented by ethnographer Sharyn Davies); and then to Albania, where sworn virgins take an oath to live and act as men. http://channel.nationalgeographic.com/channel/taboo/videos/the-third-sex/. There is also a 3-minute clip about the five genders in Indonesia on YouTube: http://www.youtube.com/watch?v=K9VmLJ3niVo.

Two-Spirit People: The Berdache Tradition in Native American Culture. Directors, Lory Levy, Michel Beauchemin, and Gretchen Vogel. 1991. Color. 23 minutes. An informative and positive view of Native American two-spirit roles, using interviews, historical photographs, and dramatic reenactments. Available online: www.frameline.org/now-showing/frameline-voices/two-spirit-people. Also available on YouTube: www.youtube.com/watch?v=8JcmAoderl4.

You Don't Know Dick. Producers, Candace Schmerhorn and Bestor Cram. 1997. 58 minutes. An intelligent assembly of interviews with six "transpeople"—female-to-male transsexuals—each of whom tells a fascinating story about the challenges in constructing a new identity. Distributed by and available from Berkeley Media LLC, www.berkeleymedia.com/catalog/berkeleymedia/films/womens_studies_gender_issues/you_don't_know_dick.

References

*denotes ethnographies particularly appropriate for students for further research

Albers, Patricia C. 1989. "From Illusion to Illumination: Anthropological Studies of American Indian Women." In *Gender and Anthropology: Critical Reviews for Research and Teaching*, edited by Sandra Morgen. Washington, DC: American Anthropological Association.

Amadiume, Ifi. 1987. *Male Daughters, Female Husbands*. Atlantic Highlands, NJ: Zed Books.

Angier, Natalie. 1997. "New Debate over Surgery on Genitals." *New York Times*, May 13, p. C1.

Anson, John. 1974. "The Female Transvestite in Early Monasticism: The Origin and Development of a Motif." *Viator: Medieval and Renaissance Studies* 5: 1–32.

Bakshi, Sandeep. 2004. "A Comparative Analysis of Hijras and Drag Queens: The Subversive Possibilities and Limits of Parading Effeminacy and Negotiating Masculinity." *Journal of Homosexuality* 46 (3/4):211–223.

Bennett, Linda Rae and Sharyn Graham Davies. 2014. *Sex and Sexualities in Indonesia: Sexual Politics, Diversity, Representations and Health*. London: Routledge.

Besnier, Niko. 1996. "Polynesian Gender Liminality through Time and Space." In *Third Sex, Third Gender: Beyond Sexual Dimorphism in Culture and History*, edited by Gilbert Herdt, pp. 285–328. New York: Zone (MIT).

———. 1997. "Sluts and Superwomen: The Politics of Gender Liminality in Urban Tonga." *Ethnos* 62 (1–2):5–31.

———. 2011. *On the Edge of the Global: Modern Anxieties in a Pacific Island Nation*. Stanford, CA: Stanford University Press.

Besnier, Niko, and Alexeyeff, Kalissa, eds. In press. *Gender on the Edge: Transgender, Gay and Other Pacific Islanders*. Honolulu, HA: University of Hawai'i Press.

Blackwood, Evelyn. 1984. "Sexuality and Gender in Certain Native American Tribes: The Case of Cross-Gender Females." *Signs: Journal of Women in Culture and Society* 10: 1–42.

———. 1998. "*Tombois* in West Sumatra: Constructing Masculinity and Erotic Desire." *Cultural Anthropology* 13 (4):491–521.

———. 2005. "Gender Transgression in Colonial and Postcolonial Indonesia." *The Journal of Asian Studies* 64 (4):849–879.

———. 2010. *Falling into the Lesbi World: Desire and Difference in Indonesia.* Honolulu, HA: University of Hawai'i Press.

Blackwood, Evelyn, and Saskia E. Wieringa. 1999. *Female Desires: Same-Sex Relations and Transgender Practices across Cultures.* New York: Columbia University Press.*

Boellstorff, Tom. 2003. "Dubbing Culture: Indonesian Gay and Lesbi Subjectivities and Ethnography in an Already Globalized World." *American Ethnologist* 30 (2):225–242.

———. 2004a. "Playing Back the Nation: Waria, Indonesian Transvestites." *Cultural Anthropology* 19 (2):159–195.

———. 2004b. "The Emergence of Political Homophobia in Indonesia: Masculinity and National Belonging." *Ethnos* 69 (4):465–486.

———. 2005a. *The Gay Archipelago.* Princeton: Princeton University Press.

———. 2005b. "Between Religion and Desire: Being Muslim and Gay in Indonesia." *American Anthropologist* 107 (4):575–585.

Bolin, Anne. 1988. *In Search of Eve: Transsexual Rites of Passage.* South Hadley, MA: Bergin and Garvey.*

———. 1996a. "Transcending and Transgendering: Male-to-Female Transsexuals, Dichotomy and Diversity." In *Third Sex, Third Gender: Beyond Sexual Dimorphism in Culture and History,* edited by Gilbert Herdt, pp. 447–486. New York: Zone (MIT).

———. 1996b. "Traversing Gender: Cultural Context and Gender Practices." In *Gender Reversals and Gender Cultures,* edited by Sabrina Petra Ramet, pp. 22–51. London and New York: Routledge.

Brandes, Stanley. 1981. "Like Wounded Stags: Male Sexual Ideology in an Andalusian Town." In *Sexual Meanings: The Cultural Construction of Gender and Sexuality,* edited by Sherry B. Ortner and Harriet Whitehead, pp. 216–239. Cambridge: Cambridge University Press.

Brownell, Susan, and Niko Besnier. 2013. "Gender and Sexuality." In *Handbook of Sociocultural Anthropology,* edited by James G. Carrier and Deborah B. Gewertz, pp. 239–258. London: Bloomsbury.

Buchanan, Scott, ed. 1977. *The Portable Plato.* New York, Penguin.

Bullough, Vern L., and Bonnie Bullough. 1993. *Cross Dressing, Sex, and Gender.* Philadelphia: University of Pennsylvania Press.

Butler, Judith. 1990. *Gender Trouble: Feminism and the Subversion of Identity.* New York and London: Routledge.

Callender, Charles, and Lee M. Kochems. 1983. "The North American Berdache." *Current Anthropology* 24 (4):443–456 (Commentary, pp. 456–470).

Cannell, Fenella. 1995. "The Power of Appearances: Beauty, Mimicry and Transformation in Bicol." In *Discrepant Histories: Translocal Essays on Filipino Cultures,* edited by V. Rafael. Manila: Anvil Publishing.

———. 1999. *Power and Intimacy in the Christian Philippines.* Cambridge: Cambridge University Press.

Chodorow, Nancy. 1974. "Family Structure and Feminine Personality." In *Women, Culture, and Society,* edited by M. Rosaldo and L. Lamphere, pp. 43–66. Stanford: Stanford University Press.

Cohen, Colleen Ballerino, Richard Wilk, and Beverly Stoeltje, eds. 1996. *Beauty Queens on the Global Stage: Gender, Contests, and Power.* New York: Routledge.

Cohen, Lawrence. 1995. "The Pleasures of Castration: The Postoperative Status of Hijras, Jankhas and Academics." In *Sexual Nature, Sexual Culture,* edited by Paul R. Abramson and Steven D. Pinkerton, pp. 276–304. Chicago: University of Chicago Press.

Connor, Randy P. 1996. *Blossom of Bone.* San Francisco: Harper.

Cornwall, Andrea. 1994. "Gendered Identities and Gender Ambiguity among Travestís in Salvador, Brazil." In *Dislocating Masculinity: Comparative Ethnographies,* edited by Andrea Cornwall and Nancy Lindisfarne, pp. 111–32. London: Routledge.

Costa, LeeRay, and Andrew Matzner. 2007. *Male Bodies, Women's Souls: Personal Narratives of Thailand's Transgendered Youth.* New York: The Haworth Press.*

Cotton, Trystan, ed. 2012. *Transgender Migrations: The Bodies, Borders, and Politics of Transition*. New York: Routledge.

Currah, Paisley, and Susan Stryker, eds. 2014. *TSQ: Transgender Studies Quarterly*. Durham, NC: Duke University Press.

Davies, Sharyn Graham. 2007. *Challenging Gender Norms: Five Genders among the Bugis in Indonesia*. Belmont, CA: Wadsworth/Thomson (now Cengage).*

———. 2010. *Gender Diversity in Indonesia: Sexuality, Islam and Queer Selves*. London: Routledge.

Devereux, George. 1937. "Institutionalized Homosexuality of the Mohave Indians." *Human Biology* 9: 498–587.

Dreger, Alice Domurat. 1998. *Hermaphrodites and the Medical Invention of Sex*. Cambridge: Harvard University Press.

Elliston, Deborah A. 1999. "Negotiating Transitional Sexual Economies: Female Māhū and Same-Sex Sexuality in 'Tahiti and Her Islands.'" In *Female Desires: Same-Sex Relations and Transgender Practices Across Cultures*, edited by Evelyn Blackwood and Saskia E. Wieringa, pp. 230–252. New York: Columbia University Press.

Errington, S. 1990. "Recasting Sex, Gender and Power: Theoretical Introduction and Regional Overview." In *Power and Difference: Gender in Island Southeast Asia*, edited by Jane Atkinson ad Shelly Errington. Stanford, CA: Stanford University Press.

Fausto-Sterling, Anne. 2000. *Sexing the Body: Gender Politics and the Construction of Sexuality*. New York: Basic Books.

Feinberg, Leslie. 1996. *Transgender Warriors: Making History from Joan of Arc to RuPaul*. Boston: Beacon.*

Fry, Peter. 1986. "Male Homosexuality and Spirit Possession in Brazil." In *Anthropology and Homosexual Behavior*, edited by Evelyn Blackwood, pp. 137–154. New York and London: Haworth Press.

———. 1995. "Male Homosexuality and Afro-Brazilian Possession Cults." In *Latin American Male Homosexualities*, edited by Stephen O. Murray, pp. 193–220. Albuquerque: University of New Mexico.

Fuller, Thomas. 2013. "Thais Cast a Wide Net for Diverse Tourists: Courting Gay and Muslim Travelers." *New York Times*, August 4, A12.

Fulton, Robert, and Steven W. Anderson. 1992. "The Amerindian 'Man-Woman': Gender, Liminality, and Cultural Continuity." *Current Anthropology* 33 (5):603–610.

Garber, Majorie. 1992. *Vested Interests: Cross-Dressing and Cultural Anxiety*. New York: Routledge, Chapman, and Hall.*

Garcia, Neil C. 1996. *Philippine Gay Culture: The Last 30 Years: Binabae to Bakla, Silahis to MSM*. Quezon City, Philippines: University of the Philippines Press.

Gaudio, Rudolf Pell. 2009. *Allah Made Us: Sexual Outlaws in an Islamic African Society*. West Sussex, UK: Wiley-Blackwell.*

Gilmore, David D. 1990. *Manhood in the Making: Cultural Concepts of Masculinity*. New Haven: Yale University Press.

———. 1996. "Above and Below: Toward a Social Geometry of Gender." *American Anthropologist* 98 (1):34–66.

Goffman, Erving. 1963. *Stigma: Notes on the Management of Spoiled Identity*. Englewood Cliffs, NJ: Prentice-Hall.

Greenberg, Julie A. 2012. *Intersexuality and the Law: Why Sex Matters*. New York: New York University Press.

Gregg, Joan. 1997. *Devils, Women, and Jews: Reflections of the Other in Medieval Sermon Stories*. Albany: State University of New York.

Gremaux, Rene. 1996. "Woman Becomes Man in the Balkans." In *Third Sex, Third Gender: Beyond Sexual Dimorphism in Culture and History*, edited by Gilbert Herdt, pp. 241–284. New York: Zone (MIT).

Hall, Kira. 1995. "Hijra/Hijrin: Language and Gender Identity." Unpublished doctoral dissertation in Linguistics, University of California, Berkeley. Ann Arbor, MI: UMI Dissertation Services.

———. 1997. "'Go Suck Your Husband's Sugarcane!': Hijras and the Use of Sexual Insult." In *Queerly Phrased: Language, Gender, and Sexuality*, edited by Anna Livia and Kira Hall, pp. 430–460. New York: Oxford.

Hayes, Kelley. 1996. *Meu Querido Viado: Gender and Possession Trance in Candomble.* Unpublished ms.

Hekma, Gert. 1996. "'A Female Soul in a Male Body': Sexual Inversion as Gender Inversion in Nineteenth-Century Sexology." In *Third Sex, Third Gender: Beyond Sexual Dimorphism in Culture and History*, edited by Gilbert Herdt, pp. 212–240. New York: Zone (MIT).

Herdt, Gilbert. 1981. *Guardians of the Flutes: Idioms of Masculinity.* New York: McGraw Hill.*

———. 1996a. "Introduction: Third Sexes and Third Genders." In *Third Sex, Third Gender: Beyond Sexual Dimorphism in Culture and History*, edited by Gilbert Herdt, pp. 21–81. New York: Zone (MIT).

———. 1996b. "Mistaken Sex: Culture, Biology and the Third Sex in New Guinea." In *Third Sex, Third Gender: Beyond Sexual Dimorphism in Culture and History*, edited by Gilbert Herdt, pp. 419–446. New York: Zone (MIT).

Hill, Willard W. 1935. "The Status of the Hermaphrodite and Transvestite in Navaho Culture." *American Anthropologist* 37: 273–279.

Hiltelbeitel, Alf. 1980. "Siva, the Goddess, and the Disguises of the Pandavas and Draupadi." *History of Religions* 20 (1–2):147–74.

Hossain, Adnan. 2012a. "Beyond Emasculation: Being Muslim and Becoming Hijra in South Asia." *Asian Studies Review* 36: 495–513.

———. 2012b. "Beyond Emasculation: Pleasure, Power and Masculinity in the Making of Hijrahood in Bangladesh." Doctoral dissertation, University of Hull, UK.

Humes, Cynthia Ann. 1996. "Becoming Male: Salvation through Gender Modification in Hinduism and Buddhism." In *Gender Reversals and Gender Cultures: Anthropological and Historical Perspectives*, edited by Sabrina Petra Ramet, pp. 123–137. London: Routledge,

Jacobs, Sue-Ellen, Wesley Thomas, and Sabine Lang, eds. 1997. *Two-Spirit People: Native American Gender Identity, Sexuality, and Spirituality.* Urbana and Chicago: University of Illinois Press.

Jackson, Peter. 1997a. "*Kathoey* >< Gay >< Man: The Historical Emergence of Gay Male Identity in Thailand." In *Sites of Desire: Economies of Pleasure: Sexualities in Asia and the Pacific*, edited by Lenore Manderson and Margaret Jolly, pp. 166–190. Chicago: University of Chicago Press.

———. 1997b. "Thai Research on Male Homosexuality and Transgenderism and the Cultural Limits of Foucaultian Analysis." *Journal of the History of Sexuality* 8 (1):52–85.

———. 1995. *Dear Uncle Go: Male Homosexuality in Thailand*. Bangkok: Bua.

Johnson, Mark. 1996. "Negotiating Style and Mediating Beauty: Transvestite (*Gay/ Bantut*) Beauty Contests in the Southern Philippines." In *Beauty Queens on the Global Stage: Gender, Contests, and Power*, edited by Colleen Ballerino Cohen, Richard Wilk, and Beverly Stoeltje, pp. 89–104. New York: Routledge.

———. 1997. *Beauty and Power: Transgendering and Cultural Transformation in the Southern Philippines.* New York: Berg.*

Karkazis, Katrina. 2008. *Intersex, Medical Authority, and Lived Experience.* Durham, NC: Duke University Press.*

Kessler, Suzanne J. 1998. *Lessons from the Intersexed.* Piscataway, NJ: Rutgers University Press.

Kessler, Suzanne J., and Wendy McKenna. 1978. *Gender: An Ethnomethodological Approach.* New York: Wiley.

Kottak, Conrad. 1990. "Hidden Women, Public Men—Public Women, Hidden Men." In *Gender Transformations*, edited by Janise Hurtig and Kate Gillogly, pp. 57–60. *Michigan Discussions in Anthropology* 9, Spring. Ann Arbor, MI.

Kulick, Don. 1996. "Causing a Commotion: Scandal as Resistance among Brazilian Travestí Prostitutes." *Anthropology Today* 12 (6):3–7.

———. 1997. "The Gender of Brazilian Transgendered Prostitutes." *American Anthropologist* 99 (3):574–585.

———. 1998. *Travestí: Sex, Gender and Culture among Brazilian Transgendered Prostitutes*. Chicago: University of Chicago Press.*

Landes, Ruth. 1946. *The City of Women*. New York: Macmillan.

Lang, Sabine. 1996. "There Is More than Just Men and Women: Gender Variance in North America." In *Gender Reversals and Gender Culture*, edited by Sabrina Petra Ramet, pp. 183–196. London and New York: Routledge

———. 1998. *Men as Women, Women as Men: Changing Gender in Native American Cultures*. Trans. from the German by John L. Vantine. Austin: University of Texas Press.

Lannoy, Richard. 1975. *The Speaking Tree*. New York: Oxford University Press.

Laqueur, Thomas. 1990. *Making Sex: Body and Gender from the Greeks to Freud*. Cambridge, MA: Harvard University Press.

Levy, Robert. 1973. *Tahitians: Mind and Experience in the Society Islands*. Chicago: University of Chicago Press.*

Lothstein, Leslie Martin. 1983. *Female-to-Male Transsexualism: Historical, Clinical and Theoretical Issues*. Boston: Routledge and Kegan Paul.

Mageo, Jeannette Marie. 1992. "Male Transvestism and Cultural Change in Samoa." *American Ethnologist* 9 (3):443–459.

Magerl, Gabriela. 2000. "Waria: A Third Gender in Indonesia." M.A. thesis, Faculty of Social Anthropology, University of Vienna, Austria.

Manalansan, Martin F. IV. 1995. "Speaking of AIDS: Language and the Filipino 'Gay' Experience in America." In *Discrepant Histories: Translocal Essays on Filipino Cultures*, edited by Vicente L. Rafael. Philadelphia: Temple University Press.

———. 1997. "In the Shadows of Stonewall: Examining Gay Transnational Politics and the Diasporic Dilemma." In *The Politics of Culture in the Shadow of Capital*, edited by Lisa Lowe and David Lloyd, pp. 485–585. Durham, NC: Duke University Press.

———. 2003. *Global Divas: Filipino Gay Men in the Diaspora*. Durham, NC: Duke University Press.

Marcos, Sylvia. 2002. "Beyond Binary Categories: Mesoamerican Religious Sexuality." In *Religion and Sexuality in Cross-Cultural Perspective*, edited by Stephen Ellingson and M. Christian Green, pp 111–136. New York: Routledge.

Mascia-Lees, Frances E. 2010. *Gender and Difference in a Globalizing World*. Long Grove, IL: Waveland Press.

Matory, J. Lorand. 1994. *Sex and the Empire That Is No More: Gender and the Politics of Metaphor in Oyo Yoruba Religion*. Minneapolis: University of Minnesota Press.

———. 1996. *Man in the City of Women*. Unpublished ms.

Matzner, Andrew. 2001. *'O Au No Keia: Voices from Hawai'i's Mahu and Transgender Communities*. USA:XLibris (www.Xlibris.com).*

Mead, Margaret. 1971. *Coming of Age in Samoa*. New York: Morrow.

Medicine, Beatrice. 1983. "Warrior Women: Sex Role Alternatives for Plains Indian Women." In *The Hidden Half: Studies of Plains Indian Women*, edited by P. Albers and B. Medicine, pp. 267–280. Lanham Park, MD: University Press of America.

Money, John, and Anke A. Ehrhardt. 1972. *Man and Woman, Boy and Girl*. Baltimore, MD: Johns Hopkins University Press.

Morris, R. C. 1994. "Three Sexes and Four Sexualities: Redressing the Discourses on Sexuality and Gender in Thailand." *Positions* 2 (1):15–43.

Munroe, Robert L., and Ruth H. Munroe. 1977. "Male Transvestism and Subsistence Economy." *Journal of Social Psychology* 103: 307–308.

Munroe, Robert L., John W. M. Whiting, and David J. Hally. 1969. "Institutionalized Male Transvestism and Sex Distinction." *American Anthropologist* 71: 87–91.

Murray, Laura Rena. 2011. "The High Price of Looking Like a Woman." *New York Times*, August 21, MB 1.

Murray, Stephen O. 1995. *Latin American Male Homosexualities*. Albuquerque: University of New Mexico Press.

Murray, Stephen O., and Will Roscoe. 1997. *Islamic Homosexualities: Culture, History, and Literature*. New York: New York University Press.

Najmabadi, Afsaneh. 2008. "Transing and Transpassing across Sex Gender Lines in Contemporary Iran." *Women's Studies Quarterly* 36 (3-4):23–42. http://nrs.harvard.edu/urn-3:HUL.InstRepos:2450776. Accessed December 5, 2013.

Nanda, Serena. 1996. "Hijras: An Alternative Sex and Gender Role in India." In *Third Sex, Third Gender: Beyond Sexual Dimorphism in Culture and History*, edited by Gilbert Herdt, pp. 373–418. New York: Zone (MIT).

———. 1999. *The Hijras of India: Neither Man nor Woman*, 2nd. ed. Belmont, CA: Wadsworth.*

———. 2010. "Life on the Margins: A Hijra's Story." In *Everyday Life in South Asia*, 2nd ed., edited by Diane P. Mines and Sarah Lamb. Bloomington: Indiana University Press.

Nanda, Serena and Joan Gregg. 2009. *Gift of a Bride: A Tale of Anthropology, Marriage, and Murder.* Lanham, MD: Altamira/Rowman and Littlefield.*

Newton, Esther. 1979. *Mother Camp: Female Impersonators in America*. Chicago: University of Chicago Press.*

Norgren, Jill, and Serena Nanda. 2006. *American Cultural Pluralism and Law*. 3rd ed. Westport, CT: Praeger.

Noor, Basittanti. 2012. "Transnational Love, Migration, and Kinship: Gay and Transgender Indonesians in the Netherlands and Belgium." MA Thesis, Department of Sociology and Anthropology, University of Amsterdam.

Oboler, Regina Smith. 1980. "Is the Female Husband a Man? Woman/Woman Marriage among the Nandi of Kenya." *Ethnology* 19 (1):69–88.

Oetomo, Dede. 1996. "Gender and Sexual Orientation in Indonesia." In *Fantasizing the Feminine in Indonesia*, edited by Laurie Sears, pp. 259–269. Durham, NC: Duke University Press.

———. 2000. "Masculinity in Indonesia: Genders, Sexualities, and Identities in a Changing Society." In *Framing the Sexual Subject: The Politics of Gender, Sexuality, and Power*, edited by Richard Parker, Regina Maria Barbosa, and Peter Aggleton. Berkeley: University of California Press.

O'Flaherty, Wendy Doniger. 1973. *Siva: The Erotic Ascetic*. New York: Oxford.

———. 1980. *Women, Androgynes, and Other Mythical Beasts*. Chicago: University of Chicago Press.

Ostor, Akos, Lina Fruzetti, and Steve Barnett, eds. 1982. *Concepts of Person: Kinship, Caste, and Marriage in India*. Cambridge, MA: Harvard University Press.

Paper Dolls. 2006. Tomer Heymann, director. Distributed by Strand Releasing.*

Parker, Richard C. 1991. *Bodies, Pleasure, and Passions: Sexual Culture in Contemporary Brazil*. Boston: Beacon Press.

———. 1995. "Changing Brazilian Constructions of Homosexuality." In *Latin American Male Homosexualities*, edited by Stephen O. Murray, pp. 241–255. Albuquerque: University of New Mexico Press,

———. 1999. "'Within Four Walls': Brazilian Sexual Culture and HIV/AIDS." In *Culture, Society and Sexuality*, edited by Richard Parker and Peter Aggleton, pp. 253–266. London: UCL Press.

Peacock, James. 1987. *Rites of Modernization: Symbolic Aspects of Indonesian Proletarian Drama*. Chicago: University of Chicago Press.

Peletz, Michael G. 2009. *Gender Pluralism: Southeast Asia Since Early Modern Times*. New York: Routledge.

Pfeffer, Georg 1995. "Manliness in the Punjab: Male Sexuality and the Khusra." *Sociologus: A Journal for Empirical Ethno-Sociology and Ethnopsychology* 45: 26–39.

Penrose, Walter. 2001. "Hidden in History: Female Homoeroticism and Women of a 'Third Nature' in the South Asian Past." *Journal of the History of Sexuality* 10 (1):3–39.

Peters, Jill. 2013. Jill Peters Photography. Jillpetersphotography.com/. Accessed September 25.

Phillimore, Peter. 1991. "Unmarried Women of the Dhaula Dhar: Celibacy and Social Control in Northwest India." *Journal of Anthropological Research* 47 (3):331–350.

Preston, Laurence W. 1987. "A Right to Exist: Eunuchs and the State in Nineteenth-Century India." *Modern Asian Studies* 21 (2):371–387.

Quinn, Naomi, and Wendy Luttrell. 2004. "Psychodynamic Universals, Cultural Particulars in Feminist Anthropology: Rethinking Hua Gender Beliefs." *Ethos* 32 (4):493–513.

Rais, Haniya. 1993. "The Socio-Economic Organization of the Khusra Community of Rawalpindi." MS thesis, the Department of Anthropology, Quaid-e-Azam University, Islamabad.

Ranade, S. N. 1983. *A Study of Eunuchs in Delhi*. Unpublished ms. Government of India, Delhi.

Reddy, Gayatri. 2005. *With Respect to Sex: Negotiating Hijra Identity in South India*. Chicago: University of Chicago Press.

———. 2006. "The Bonds of Love: Companionate Marriage and the Desire for Intimacy among Hijras in Hyderabad, India." In *Modern Loves: The Anthropology of Romantic Courtship & Companionate Marriage*, edited by Jennifer S. Hirsch and Holly Wardlow. Ann Arbor: University of Michigan Press.

———. 2010. "Crossing 'Lines' of Difference: Transnational Movements and Sexual Subjectivities in Hyderabad, India." In *Everyday Life in South Asia*, 2nd ed., edited by Diane P. Mines and Sarah Lamb, pp. 132–143. Bloomington: University of Indiana Press.

Reis, Elizabeth. 2009. *Bodies in Doubt: An American History of Intersex*. Baltimore, MD. Johns Hopkins University Press.

Roscoe, Will. 1991. *The Zuni Man-Woman*. Albuquerque: University of New Mexico Press.*

———. 1995. "Cultural Anesthesia and Lesbian and Gay Studies." *American Anthropologist* 97 (3):448–452.

———. 1996. "How to Become a Berdache: Toward a Unified Analysis of Gender Diversity." In *Third Sex, Third Gender: Beyond Sexual Dimorphism in Culture and History*, edited by Gilbert Herdt, pp. 329–372. New York: Zone (MIT).

———. 1998. *Changing Ones: Third and Fourth Genders in Native North America*. London: Macmillan.

Roscoe, Will, and Stephen O. Murray, eds. 1998. *Boy-Wives and Female-Husbands: Studies in African Homosexualities*. New York: St. Martins.

Schaeffer, Claude E. 1965. "The Kutenai Female Berdache: Courier, Guide, Prophetess, and Warrior." *Ethnohistory: The Bulletin of the Ohio Valley Historic Indian Conference* 12 (3):173–236.

Shakhsari, Sima. 2013. "Shuttling Between Bodies and Borders: Transmigration and the Politics of Rightful Killing." In *Transgender Studies Reader II*, edited by Aren Aizura and Susan Stryker. New York: Routledge.

Shapiro, Judith. 1991. "Transsexualism: Gender and the Mutability of Sex." In *Body Guards: The Cultural Politics of Gender Ambiguity*, edited by Julia Epstein and Kristina Straub, pp. 248–278. New York: Routledge.

Shore, Bradd. 1981. "Sexuality and Gender in Samoa: Conceptions and Missed Conceptions." In *Sexual Meanings: The Cultural Construction of Gender and Sexuality*, edited by Sherry B. Ortner and Harriet Whitehead, pp. 192–215. Cambridge: Cambridge University Press.

Thomas, Wesley. 1997. "Navajo Cultural Constructions of Gender and Sexuality." In *Two-Spirit People: Native American Gender Identity, Sexuality, and Spirituality*, edited by Sue-Ellen Jacobs, Wesley Thomas, and Sabine Lang, pp. 156–173. Urbana and Chicago: University of Illinois Press.

Trumbach, Randolph. 1996. "London's Sapphists: From Three Sexes to Four Genders in the Making of Modern Culture." In *Third Sex, Third Gender: Beyond Sexual Dimorphism in Culture and History*, edited by Gilbert Herdt, pp. 111–136. New York: Zone (MIT).

——. 1998. *Sex and the Gender Revolution*. Vol. 1 of *Heterosexuality and the Third Gender in Enlightenment London*. Chicago: University of Chicago Press.

Turner, Victor. 1969. *The Ritual Process: Structure and Anti-structure*. Ithaca, NY: Cornell University Press.

Valentine, David. 2007. *Imagining Transgender: An Ethnography of a Category*. Durham, NC: Duke University Press.

Wafer, James. 1991. *The Taste of Blood: Spirit Possession in Brazilian Candomble*. Philadelphia: University of Pennsylvania Press.

Whitam, Frederick L. 1992. "Bayot and Callboy: Homosexual-Heterosexual Relations in the Philippines." In *Oceanic Homosexualities*, edited by Stephen O. Murray, pp. 231–248. New York: Garland.

Whitehead, Harriet. 1981. "The Bow and the Burden Strap: A New Look at Institutionalized Homosexuality in Native North America." In *Sexual Meanings: The Cultural Construction of Gender and Sexuality*, edited by Sherry B. Ortner and Harriet Whitehead, pp. 80–115. Cambridge: Cambridge University Press.

Wieringa, Saskia E. 2008. "'If there is no feeling . . .': The Dilemma between Silence and Coming Out in a Working-Class Butch/Femme Community in Jakarta. In *Love and Globalization: Transformations of Intimacy in the Contemporary World*, edited by Mark B. Padilla, Jennifer S. Hirsch, Miguel Munoz-Laboy, Robert E. Sember, and Richard G. Parker, pp. 70–89. Nashville, TN: Vanderbilt University Press.

Wikan, Unni. 1977. "Man Becomes Woman: Transsexualism in Oman as a Key to Gender Roles." *Man* 12: 304–319.

Williams, Patricia J. 2011. "Gender Trouble." *The Nation*, May 23, p. 9.

Williams, Walter. 1992. *The Spirit and the Flesh: Sexual Diversity in American Indian Culture*. Boston: Beacon.*

Winter, Sam. 2013. www.TransgenderASIA.org. Accessed October 19.

Xian, Kathryn. 2001. *Ke Kulana He Mahu: Remembering a Sense of Place*. Film, see Selected Films list.

Zhang, Michael. 2012. "Portraits of Albanian Women Who Have Lived Their Lives as Man." Petapixel.com/2012/12/26 (also available on jillpetersphotography.com).

Zwilling, L., and M. Sweet. 1996. "Like a City Ablaze: The Third Sex and the Creation of Sexuality in Jain Religious Literature." *Journal of the History of Sexuality* 6 (3):359–384.

——. 2000. "The Evolution of Third Sex Constructs in Ancient India: A Study in Ambiguity." In *Constructing Ideologies: Religion, Gender, and Social Definition in India*, edited by Julia Leslie, pp. 99–133. Delhi: Oxford University Press.

Index

141